instant manager
skills for success

CMI

managing
CHANGE

BERNICE WALMSLEY

HODDER
EDUCATION
LIVRE UK

The publisher has used its best endeavours to ensure that the URLs for external websites referred to in this book are correct and active at the time of going to press. However, the publisher and the author have no responsibility for the websites and can make no guarantee that a site will remain live or that the content will remain relevant, decent or appropriate.

Orders: Please contact Bookpoint Ltd, 130 Milton Park, Abingdon, Oxon OX14 4SB. Telephone: (44) 01235 827720, Fax: (44) 01235 400454. Lines are open from 9.00 to 5.00, Monday to Saturday, with a 24-hour message answering service. You can also order through our website www.hoddereducation.co.uk.

British Library Cataloguing in Publication Data
A catalogue record for this title is available from the British Library.

ISBN-13: 978 0340 94734 0

First published   2009
Impression number   10 9 8 7 6 5 4 3 2 1
Year   2012 2011 2010 2009

Typeset by Transet Limited, Coventry, England.
Printed in Great Britain for Hodder Education, an Hachette Livre UK Company, 338 Euston Road, London NW1 3BH, by Cox & Wyman, Reading, Berkshire RG1 8EX.

Hachette Livre UK's policy is to use papers that are natural, renewable and recyclable products and made from wood grown in sustainable forests. The logging and manufacturing processes are expected to conform to the environmental regulations of the country of origin.

The Chartered Management Institute

CMI

The Chartered Management Institute is the only chartered professional body that is dedicated to management and leadership. We are committed to raising the performance of business by championing management.

We represent 80,000 individual managers and have 450 corporate members. Within the Institute there are also a number of distinct specialisms, including the Institute of Business Consulting and Women in Management Network.

We exist to help managers tackle the management challenges they face on a daily basis by raising the standard of management in the UK. We are here to help individuals become better managers and companies develop better managers.

We do this through a wide range of products and services, from practical management checklists to tailored training and qualifications. We produce research on the latest 'hot' management issues, provide a vast array of useful information through our online management information centre, as well as offering consultancy services and career information.

You can access these resources 'off the shelf' or we can provide solutions just for you. Our range of products and services is designed to ensure organisations and managers develop their potential and excel. Whether you are at the start of your career or a proven performer in the boardroom, we have something for you.

We engage policy makers and opinion formers and, as the leading authority on management, we are regularly consulted on a range of management issues. Through our in-depth research and regular policy surveys of members, we have a deep understanding of the latest management trends.

For more information visit our website **www.managers.org.uk** or call us on **01536 207307**.

Chartered Manager

Transform the way you work

The Chartered Management Institute's Chartered Manager award is the ultimate accolade for practising professional managers. Designed to transform the way you think about your work and how you add value to your organisation, it is based on demonstrating measurable impact.

This unique award proves your ability to make a real difference in the workplace.

Chartered Manager focuses on the six vital business skills of:

- Leading people
- Managing change
- Meeting customer needs
- Managing information and knowledge
- Managing activities and resources
- Managing yourself

Transform your organisation

There is a clear and well-established link between good management and improved organisational performance. Recognising this, the Chartered Manager scheme requires individuals to demonstrate how they are applying their leadership and change management skills to make significant impact within their organisation.

Transform your career

Whatever career stage a manager is at Chartered Manager will set them apart. Chartered Manager has proven to be a stimulus to career progression, either via recognition by their current employer or through the motivation to move on to more challenging roles with new employers.

But don't take just our word for it ...

Chartered Manager has transformed the careers and organisations of managers in all sectors.

- *'Being a Chartered Manager was one of the main contributing factors which led to my recent promotion.'*
  Lloyd Ross, Programme Delivery Manager, British Nuclear Fuels

- *'I am quite sure that a part of the reason for my success in achieving my appointment was due to my Chartered Manager award which provided excellent, independent evidence that I was a high quality manager.'*
  Donaree Marshall, Head of Programme Management Office, Water Service, Belfast

- *'The whole process has been very positive, giving me confidence in my strengths as a manager but also helping me to identify the areas of my skills that I want to develop. I am delighted and proud to have the accolade of Chartered Manager.'*
  Allen Hudson, School Support Services Manager, Dudley Metropolitan County Council

- *'As we are in a time of profound change, I believe that I have, as a result of my change management skills, been able to provide leadership to my staff. Indeed, I took over three teams and carefully built an integrated team, which is beginning to perform really well. I believe that the process I went through to gain Chartered Manager status assisted me in achieving this and consequently was of considerable benefit to my organisation.'*
  George Smart, SPO and D/Head of Resettlement, HM Prison Swaleside

To find out more or to request further information please visit our website **www.managers.org.uk/cmgr** or call us on **01536 207429**.

Contents

CHAPTER 03

CHAPTER 04

CHAPTER 05

CHAPTER 06

CHAPTER 07

CHAPTER 08

CHAPTER 09

CHAPTER 10

CHAPTER 11

CHAPTER 12

Foreword

There has never been a greater need for better management and leadership skills in the UK. As we've seen over the past couple of years, it's all too often the case that management incompetence takes the blame for high-profile, costly and sometimes tragic failures. Put this in the context of a world dominated by changing technology and growing international competition, and every manager in this country has a responsibility for ensuring that he or she has the best possible skills to contribute to successful business performance.

So it is alarming that just one in five managers in the UK are professionally qualified. The truth is that we spend less on management development in the UK than our European competitors. Effectively this means that, if you want to develop professionally, if you want to boost your career chances, or if you just want recognition for the work you do, the onus is on you – the individual – to improve your skills. What it also means is that all of us – individual managers, employers and policy makers – need to answer difficult questions about how well equipped we are to lead in the 21st century. Are our standards slipping? How capable are we when it comes to meeting the skill requirements of modern business? Studies show that project management, alliance-building and communication skills are the three key 'over-arching' skills that must be mastered by the successful manager. But how many people can honestly claim they have mastery over all three?

In recent years the news has been dominated by stories focusing on breathtaking management failures. The collapse of the banking sector has been much-analysed and will continue to be discussed in the years to come. It's not just the private sector. Vast amounts of column inches have been devoted to investigations of failures across the health and social care services, too. The spotlight has also been on management, at an individual level, as the recession has deepened in the aftermath of the banking crisis, with dramatic rises in the UK's unemployment levels. Many managers are fighting an ongoing battle to control costs and survive with reduced credit and slowing demand. They are also struggling to prove their worth, to show they meet required standards now, and in the long-term.

But imagine a world where management and leadership enables top-class performance right across British businesses, the public sector and our not-for-profit organisations – where management isn't a byword for bureaucracy and failure, but plays a real role in boosting performance. The way to achieve such a realistic utopia is by developing the skills that will help you, as a manager, perform to the best of your capability. And that is why this book will help. Its aim is to provide you with practical, digestible advice that you can take straight from the pages to apply in your working environment.

Does any of this matter? Well, you wouldn't want your accounts signed off by someone lacking a financial qualification. You certainly wouldn't let an unqualified surgeon anywhere near you with a scalpel, nor would you seek an unqualified lawyer to represent your interests. Why, then, should your employer settle for management capability that is second best? It means that you need to take time out to develop your skills so that these can be evaluated and so you can stand out from the competition.

What's more, managers will play a critical role in determining how well the UK meets a wide range of challenges over the next decade. How can managers foster innovation to promote economic growth? How do they tackle the gender pay gap and the continued under-representation of women in the boardroom, as part of building truly fair, diverse organisations? Managers in all sectors will need to learn how to lead their teams through the changes we face; they will also need to be able to manage change. Above all, managers will need to grasp the nettle when it comes to managing information and knowledge. The key will rest in how they learn to manage themselves.

First-class management and leadership really can drive up both personal and corporate performance. It can boost national productivity and enhance social wellbeing. If you want to be the best manager you can be, this book is for you. In one go it will provide you with practical advice and the experience of business leaders. It is also a fascinating and enthralling read!

Ruth Spellman OBE
Chief Executive
Chartered Management Institute

Acknowledgements

Thanks must go, as ever, to my husband William for his support, patience and encouragement and to Andrew Hill of Committed Network for his help with the Gantt chart.

Grateful thanks also to Alison Frecknall and all the team at Hodder for all their friendly help and guidance during the commissioning and production of this book.

01

Introduction

Who should read this book?

If you want to upgrade your management skills, then this series of books – a sub-strand of the Instant Manager series – is for you. The series covers a range of skills needed by today's managers including those set out in the employer-led set of standards (the National Occupational Standards) for leadership and management drawn up to improve the productivity and profitability of business in the UK.

This book is for any manager – new or experienced – who needs help with making change happen in their working life. It is not jargon-filled or too complicated and theory-bound. It contains practical advice to help you in your working life. So, if you need to acquire the knowledge needed to plan change, encourage innovation and lead a change programme in your organisation then this book will help you to acquire the necessary skills.

A range of topics, linked by the common themes of improving performance in your organisation and enhancing your own skills set, will be covered in each book in the form of ten questions on the topic plus an interview with a well-known business expert. In this book you will find the answers to questions that will show you how to manage change within your organisation. There will be plenty of information and ideas on how to identify, nurture and develop ideas within your team and then how to develop the plans for change. You will then identify the best ways to lead change, while clarifying the risks associated with change and get ideas on how to keep your team motivated while change is progressing.

At the end of each chapter, after a specific question has been answered, there will be a summary of the chapter and a short action checklist, which will give you a series of practical steps you will need to take to overcome the challenge of that topic at work.

The skills that you will learn in this book are vital to your success as a manager. Of course, the skills you need are many and varied, so in this book we will be concentrating on the ones you need to encourage innovation and manage change.

What skills do you need to manage change?

Many of the skills necessary to manage change are those that all managers will need – the general skills that you will use every day. But all managers will need to make changes from time to time in order to keep up with competitors or improve existing ways of doing things, and there are specific skills that will be vital if you are to arrive at a successful outcome and decide upon and implement the changes that are necessary to improve performance in your organisation.

General management skills such as problem solving and communication will be useful in ensuring that your team know what is required of them, and more specific ones such as team building and monitoring will be vital in, for example, encouraging innovation, while decision making and leadership skills will be necessary when taking control of change implementation.

Let's look in a little more detail at the skills that will be necessary in each of the main steps to change:

- **Encouraging innovation** – the first step in making changes is to have the ideas, so creative thinking and problem solving skills will be invaluable here. You will also need to have leadership and communication skills in order to get the best ideas from your team and to develop an innovative culture within it. Encouraging innovation is a vital skill if your organisation is to keep pace in a very competitive environment. The first chapter will help you to do this.
- **Leading change** – the most obvious skill necessary to lead change is that of leadership, but you will also need to develop the skills of negotiating, influencing and motivating if you are to successfully lead a programme of change. If you are leading change, you will not be carrying out every task yourself so you will also need to learn how to delegate.
- **Planning change** – analytical skills are important when planning change and communications skills, including obtaining feedback from others involved, will also be necessary. During the planning stage of any change programme you will need to be aware of the risks involved and be able to plan how you will deal with the problems that may arise. There will be a lot of information to deal with at this stage so it is essential that you acquire – or improve – the skill of information management to equip yourself for this task.

● **Implementing change** – when putting plans for change into action you will need a wide variety of skills including those of delegating, communicating and negotiating. Along the way you will need to employ the skills of assessing and monitoring the progress and outcomes of the change plans.

After that brief overview, let's move on to the challenges that will meet you in the first of our questions, which is aimed at helping you to see what change is, what is involved and why it happens.

02

What is change?

Change can be defined as 'to make or become different' and in business usage generally refers to improvements that are being made, so change in this context must therefore be managed. Many people are resistant to change in both their business and personal lives (more about this in Chapter 7) but change is inevitable. One only has to look at the changes that have taken place in business over the past years to realise that it is a continual process and not one that can be avoided. To take just a few examples, first of all technology has been the driver of some of the biggest changes to take place in organisations throughout the world in the past few decades. These changes have caused some jobs to be lost but new ones to be created. Typists, for example, are very rarely employed these days while IT specialists are in high demand in many businesses, but less than a hundred years ago no one would have known what one of these was. Environmental changes and an increased awareness of the possible problems created has caused further changes in how business is conducted and have, in their own right, created businesses, lobbying organisations and charities. Social changes such as increased life expectancy have caused changes in pensions arrangements and in the products that are offered, such as an increased demand for retirement care facilities or holidays for people still fit enough, at an advanced age, to enjoy them.

From these few examples it can be seen that change is constant and all organisations must manage change if they are to stay in business. No matter how much we may resist change, it will happen.

As Charles Darwin said 'It is not the strongest species that survive, nor the most intelligent, but the ones that are most responsive to change', so change must be acknowledged and dealt with if we are to survive in business. For this reason, we will look in this chapter at what drives change in organisations and why we must manage it.

Reasons for change

Change is continual and will happen whatever any organisation does or doesn't do. But the reasons for some changes in organisations will have a definite cause either within the organisation or in the environment in which it operates and will mean that change is almost unavoidable. These include:

- Mergers or acquisitions – changes in management usually become necessary when organisations are merged together or are under new ownership. Changes in business methods, location and so on will often be necessary too.
- A serious business downturn – if results deteriorate most organisations will decide to do something different in an effort to reverse their fortunes – or even to ensure their survival.
- Legislative changes – if, for example, new emission targets are set for motor vehicles or minimum wage regulations are revised then changes may have to be made.

There are many other reasons for change but most require a proactive approach rather than the reactive approach which is evident in the above examples. Organisations may choose to change as a result of:

- rising costs
- a new strategy
- a sales review
- new technology becoming available

Whatever the reason for change, it will need the right approach and to be handled carefully. Knowing your own feelings about change can be helpful if you have to take part in a change programme – whether managing it or simply being a member of a team in such a situation. In the next section we will look at your attitude to change.

How do you view change?

Having read the section above, it is obvious that change is inevitable but knowing this will not necessarily make you view it in a particular way or react to it more positively. The views we hold about change are often instinctive and difficult to alter but it is essential to have a positive and realistic view of change if we, and the organisations we work in, are to prosper.

In Chapter 7 we will look more closely at what the barriers to change are and how they can be overcome, but in this chapter we are concerned with how individuals feel about change and why they may feel this way. The main feeling that people have when they encounter a possible change is one of fear. They may feel anxious that they will not be able to cope in a new situation. Uncertainty can induce fear in most people and fear can make people behave in ways which are not conducive to the success of the change that is being proposed. This fear can start with just one individual but can spread if not contained. It could almost be said to be 'contagious'. This is why, when undertaking organisational change, people's fears must be taken seriously.

Fear and uncertainty can quickly derail a change programme even when it is obvious that it is a change that is going to benefit the organisation and the people employed in it. The best way to deal with this sort of situation is by effective communication. Methods of communicating with everyone involved in, and affected by, the change, must be planned into any change programme.

So, how do you personally view change? Ask yourself if you've ever had those feelings of fear and uncertainty. Or maybe you have been faced with a change and thought 'it can't be done, it's not possible'? Or maybe you subscribe to the dictum 'if it isn't broke, don't fix it'? If you recognise yourself in any of these negative scenarios then you will need to change this negativity so that it does not get in the way of success in your current work role and in your career. Reading this book will help as it will give you the skills and tools to deal with change differently and to manage it. You will also be able to see that as change is inevitable you must accept it with a positive attitude; there are plenty of instances where change has brought about improvements. Indeed, you will see that without change nothing will get better – things will only stagnate or get worse. Change can be daunting but with the right approach and careful planning and management, it can produce improvements.

Are you completely satisfied?

Although natural instincts may sometimes preclude us from actively seeking change, we should all ask ourselves the question: 'Are we satisfied?' Could things be better? Are improvements possible? In almost every work situation, there are things that are not working at their optimum level. Maybe profits could be increased – and that is the most common reason for change in any profit-making organisation. Maybe, if you work for a non-profit making organisation, you can see that processes could be made more efficient, saving money for the organisation, or new 'customers' can be gained by changing what you are offering.

When you have got over the negative attitudes that may stop you looking for change, your next issue will be to develop an attitude for innovation. Any successful organisation will have established and nurtured a culture of innovation – and more about this in succeeding chapters.

Before any of this you will need to decide what it is that can be improved. This may be done in a variety of ways such as conducting a full review of the business, benchmarking to compare the organisation with others in your field to see where improvements could be made or by concentrating on one particular area – sales or production, for example, where improvements could produce rapid results in terms of efficiencies and profits.

The questions that need to be answered when deciding whether or not you are completely satisfied include:

- Could you make more profit? If you have even a suspicion that more profit is possible, then a full review to decide what changes to make is a must.
- Is the technology that you currently use in the organisation working to its optimum effect? Are there any IT problems? Is new technology now available that could improve your working methods?
- Are all your staff working to the best of their abilities? And do you have the right person for each job? Do you have sufficient staff? Or too many? Do any of the employees need training in any area?
- Is your customer service as good as it possibly could be? Are your customers completely satisfied every time? Do you have a high volume of customer complaints or returned goods?

- Is continuous improvement part of your organisation's culture? If not, it should be.
- Is there a 'can do' attitude in the organisation? If not, then maybe a culture change can be planned and managed.
- Do you have a mission statement and does everything you do in the organisation comply with this and uphold the values that have been set?

Sometimes, of course, it is easier to stay just where we are; to change nothing. But this will only work in the short term, as every organisation is under external pressure to change. Markets will change, customers will be lost, systems will become obsolete, products will lose their appeal and new ones will become necessary, so it is far better to take a proactive approach to change and to make change happen when you want it to happen rather than it being forced upon you. We will look in later chapters at the benefits of innovation and at how change can be directed so that it works in favour of the organisation. Let's look now at what might happen if you do nothing, and stay just as you are.

What will happen if you stay as you are?

If you are still stuck in the rut of thinking that change in your current set up is unnecessary, you would do well to consider carefully what will happen if you do nothing. It can be helpful at this stage to look at changes that have happened in your organisation or department over the past few months or years. Even if you think that there have been no changes – certainly not ones that have been planned and are part of a strategy – think carefully. For example:

- Has there been a change in the equipment that you use?
- Have you lost or gained a significant customer?
- Have you had any changes in personnel?
- Have your profits stayed exactly the same?
- Are the prices you're paying for goods that you buy in the course of business the same?
- Have there been any regulatory changes that you have had to comply with in your business?
- Is the market in which you are trading completely unchanging – or have new competitors come along or old ones dropped out?
- Are you still using all the same suppliers as you have always used?

By now you will probably be thinking that yes, changes have occurred but not ones that were planned. They just happened and you had to deal with them. That is the point that must be grasped – that changes will happen even if we want to stay the same. Some changes will always happen to us and we may have to 'fire fight' to keep the organisation stable, but other changes can be managed and more advantage gained for the organisation than if we just let them happen. For example, suppose a major supplier increases its prices. Wouldn't it be better for you to have researched the market and found an alternative supplier before this happened? Perhaps, in this case, you could have given a trial order to the new supplier.

There are disadvantages to resisting change and trying to stay as we are. Let's look at some of the things that can happen to organisations that fail to change:

- They may become less efficient.
- Their productivity will decrease.
- Valuable members of staff may leave to go somewhere more forward-thinking.
- Sales will fall.

- They will lose market share to their competitors.
- Profits will decrease.
- Their costs will increase.
- Ultimately, they will go out of business.

So, a lack of change can seriously damage an organisation. If we take one example – that of an unchanging product range – we can see that planned change is far more beneficial to the organisation. All products have a lifecycle that they will follow and if any of yours are in the later stages of this cycle then you will need to develop new ones to ensure that your business prospers and continues to grow. (What we say about products applies equally to services.) The stages that all products have to go through – from initial development through to product decline – are as follows:

- *Development* – this is when you develop the product, so the costs will be high and you will not yet have started to make a profit from this product.
- *Launch* – if you have got the product right then sales will grow rapidly from the launch and profits will be significant.
- *Growing* – at this point sales will be growing and you will be making money from the product.
- *Plateau* – this is when sales have reached their peak and further growth is not possible. It may be possible to extend the life of your product by adding new features or updating its design but developing new products should be your priority at this stage.
- *Decline* – this is when your product is, in effect, dying. Its performance is in decline, it faces competition from all sides, so prices are being driven down. New product development becomes urgent.

As product decline appears to be inevitable, it is best if new products are continually in the pipeline. This will ensure that you will have products at different stages and so will have at least one at the peak of its profitability at any time. This example shows that staying as you are is not an option and that a successful organisation will embrace change and not simply allow change to happen to it.

Change will happen whatever you try to do. It is far better to manage the change in order to maintain profitability and viability for your organisation and planned changes can bring lots of benefits to the organisation such as reduced costs when suppliers are reviewed and perhaps changed or improved productivity when business processes are improved. Later in this chapter we will look at just what constitutes change management. Before that we will look at what drives change.

The causes and drivers of change

There will always be a number of drivers of change impacting on your organisation. These could include the following.

New technology

Depending on your business, this could be new equipment or machinery becoming available, or ways of doing things that will make your product better or make it more cost effective to produce. Alternatively, it could be the technology you use to produce information rather than goods. And of course, major changes have taken place in recent decades in terms of online businesses. Very few businesses can afford to ignore the drive for an online presence and possibly for online sales to take the place of more conventional, and traditional routes to market.

Communications

This is closely allied to the changes in technology referred to above. The exponential growth in the use of communications technology such as mobile phones, emails, social networking websites and the internet both as a research tool and as a route to market in recent years has been responsible for many changes. These could affect your sales and marketing strategy as well as how you communicate with customers and suppliers and how you produce information for use in the business.

Product innovation

As discussed earlier, all products have a lifecycle and will inevitably decline in terms of profitability, so new products must always be in the pipeline.

Product improvements

The lifecycle of a product can often be extended by making minor improvements to it. This can be in response to what is happening in the market – what your competitors are offering, for example – or to what your customers are telling you they need.

Changing markets

Old competitors will inevitably drop out of the market from time to time and new ones will enter. Or it may be a more fundamental change to the market in which you operate such as a change in the way goods are sold (think of the growth in online sales, for example) or to the actual goods on offer (for example, who buys typewriters these days?).

Regulatory changes

Many industries are subject to specific regulations (the food industry, for example) but all businesses are affected by general regulatory changes that may happen, such as employment law, and cause changes that must be dealt with.

Competitiveness

The need to maintain competitiveness is ever present, so what your competitors do may demand action from you and cause changes to become necessary in your organisation.

Economic factors

During times of economic downturn or recession, demand for an organisation's products and services may decrease, so there may be a need to cut costs or review procedures to ensure that profitability is maintained.

Demographics

An ageing population brings different requirements and this may affect the product offer of an organisation or how the products are sold.

Social changes

The way people live is ever-changing. For example, there are more single-person households and one-parent families. What effect will this have on your product offer? It could also affect your personnel policies if more flexible working is demanded or if people want to work beyond retirement age for example.

Environmental factors

There is an increasing emphasis on matters such as climate change and recycling which may require a reaction from any organisation. For both social benefit and marketing purposes it may be desirable to implement a recycling project in the organisation, for example.

Global markets

If your organisation exports its products, or plans to do so in the future (or if your competitors do) changes here will have an effect on how you do business.

All of these circumstances are largely outside the control of an organisation but will usually demand a reaction from it if it is to remain profitable so, yet again, we can see that change is inevitable.

Case study

A manufacturer of paper tableware (napkins, plates, tablecloths, etc.) to supermarkets and independent shops had a policy of regularly consulting customers to find out what they really wanted and then used the results of these enquiries to change its product offering. On one such information-seeking visit to a small retailer who was closely in touch with her own customers, it was told by the retailer that she would like to see smaller pack sizes of their coloured table napkins. Although this meant that the manufacturer had to make some adjustments to its packaging routines and that costs were slightly increased, it complied with its customer's request. The result was increased sales. The manufacturer did not lose sales of the standard, larger packs but gained new users of its products when they offered small pack sizes. Its customer advised them how well the new pack size had been received by people planning a special colour theme for a dinner party and was also bought by people who did not normally buy paper napkins. The manufacturer offered the new pack size in all its coloured and luxury ranges to all its customers and the product proved to be very successful.

Identifying these drivers of change that affect your organisation is essential if you are to approach change strategically and to plan for the improvements that all businesses require to survive and prosper. Understanding what impact these drivers of change are likely to have on the organisation will enable managers to plan appropriately. They will be able to:

- make better investment decisions
- identify opportunities
- identify threats
- develop new products.

Just as there are drivers *for* change, there are drivers *against* change. Understanding this can be helpful in managing change. The writer Kurt Lewin developed a simple model to illustrate this theory:

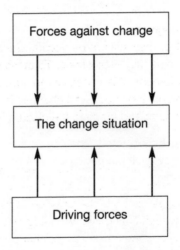

This theory helps us to analyse how change works and how we can handle change so that it works in our favour. Lewin's theory was that the situation will remain unchanged when the driving forces and restraining forces at work in a situation are equal. Driving forces that will push change along include demands from customers, positive management attitudes towards change and increased competition. Restraining forces that work against the driving forces could include the attitudes of the workforce, financial restrictions or a lack of expertise. Lewin went further in developing his theories about change by detailing three stages that he believed change went through. These are:

1. *Unfreezing* – this is where the need for change is accepted and the existing ways of doing things are dismantled or 'unfrozen'. At this stage a lot of work must be put into communication – convincing people that change is vital, what will happen if they stay as they are, what can be gained from change and so on.
2. *Changing* – this is the planning and implementation stages where actual changes take place.
3. *Refreezing* – this is where changes are consolidated. Even though changes have been made in the second stage, they may still not be accepted and new practices and systems fully established. To avoid going back to former methods, it is necessary to 'iron out' any problems and to signal the successful changes by recognising achievements and marking the closure of the change project.

Understanding this theory can assist in dealing with change in that it can be seen that for change to happen we must ensure that the pressure for change exceeds the pressure against it. If there are forces at work against change we will need either to reduce those pressures or increase the pressures for change accordingly.

For change to be successful there must be at least four conditions in place:

1. *Commitment* – pressure to change and the commitment necessary to make change happen must come from the very top of the organisation. If senior managers and/or owners and stakeholders in the organisation do not make very clear their commitment and back this up with

appropriate resources, communication and action then it is highly unlikely that the workforce will become convinced of the need for change. Without this commitment any change programme that may be implemented is likely to fail.

2. *Leadership* – there must be a clear vision from the leaders in the organisation and this vision must be effectively communicated to the workforce so that individuals 'buy in' to the process of change. If the leadership is not consistent or not sufficiently convinced itself of the need for change, then successful change will not happen.

3. *Resources* – change will not happen if the workforce responsible for making it happen do not have sufficient time allowed for the extra work and the financial resources to cover any extra expenditure on equipment, overtime, marketing and so on. These resources must be guaranteed and provided by management. Without resources, not only will employees be unable to carry out the changes but they will also be likely to put in less effort as they will undoubtedly feel that the senior managers are not sufficiently committed to the change that is being proposed.

4. *An active approach* – the leaders in the organisation must take action. There is little point in repeatedly stating that they are committed to change and giving reasons for the proposed changes (even perfectly valid reasons) if they do not back up their words with action. As we have stated, they must provide resources such as time and money, and must prepare plans, timescales and appropriate guidance for the workforce.

These four conditions – commitment, leadership, resources and action are absolutely essential before any change process will show results.

What is change management?

Change management is the taking of a proactive approach to how change is dealt with in an organisation. It involves not just adapting to the change but also spotting the need for a change within an organisation, initiating that change and then controlling it. Change management is crucial to the successful outcome of any improvement project. It ensures that any change is properly defined, planned and approved before its introduction. As we have discussed previously, if change is simply allowed to happen to an organisation then it will not deal well with the circumstances in which it finds itself. Changes will always impact upon staff and will often have knock-on effects on other parts of the system that are not overtly affected by the change. For example, a change in the IT systems used to produce invoices may make staff uncertain of what they have to do at various points in the invoicing process and so may affect their productivity until they become familiar with the new methods. Such a change may also result in invoices being sent out later than would be the case with the previous system. This in turn may extend the number of days that the organisation has to wait for payment and will ultimately affect its cashflow. If targets are in place based, for example, on the number of debtor days, then the members of staff or departments targeted in such a way will be seen as failing when, in fact, they are simply trying to cope with a change aimed at improvements. If a change of this nature had been properly planned and managed then staff could have been properly trained before 'going live' with the new system. They could also have been monitored to make sure things were going well and the new system implemented in an organised manner to avoid any cash flow problems. Change must be planned, managed and monitored.

An important part of this planning and implementation concerns communication with people within the organisation, which is essential to a successful outcome. Before any change programme is embarked upon, the plan should include details of how the change should be communicated to all involved in the process. This will help to avoid problems and should secure the cooperation of those involved. This communication plan should include the reasons for the change, what the objectives are, any timescales and regular updates on progress. There will be more on this topic in later chapters.

As change is such an inevitable and constant part of working in any organisation, and the management of that change is vital to success, then it is obvious that any manager must acquire the skills necessary to deal with it competently.

SUMMARY

In this initial chapter about change we have looked at how people view change and at how this can affect how an organisation is managed and the level of success it has. A vital part of making a success of a planned change is dealing with the attitudes and approaches to change that those involved have.

We saw that change is inevitable and constant, and that staying where you are is not a viable option. When deciding whether or not you are satisfied with the status quo, particular attention should be paid to the profitability of the organisation, the technology that is currently being used, personnel issues, levels of customer satisfaction and the culture of the organisation. Even in the unlikely event of a manager being totally satisfied with everything that an organisation does and achieves, external changes will nevertheless happen and it is therefore vital that any manager learns to deal with change so that its impact on the organisation is beneficial – or at least not allowed to be detrimental.

Finally, we looked briefly at what change management is, the need for change management in an organisation and why it is vital to the success of improvement plans.

ACTION CHECKLIST

1. Assess your own attitude to change and also that of people who report to you. Do you see any of these people – or yourself – being a particular problem? If so, think about how you can deal with the situations that may arise.
2. Can you name three examples of external changes that have affected your organisation?
3. Consider an improvement plan in which you have been involved – was it managed well, were the levels of communication with the people involved adequate?
4. Give examples of drivers of change that are currently acting upon your organisation.
5. What impact have these drivers of change had on the organisation?

03

When is change needed?

The short answer to the question 'When is change needed?' is – always. As we discussed in Chapter 2, organisations are never perfect and they should be constantly changing in order to improve. Improvements in all aspects of business, whether it is in profitability, costs, delivery times, customer satisfaction, staff performance or culture, are only ever achieved by change. Also, the events going on around all organisations must be reacted to and changes will need to be made to adjust to things going on in any market.

So, what might need to be changed? Again, there is a short answer – everything. But, to be more specific, innovations and improvements should be sought in the following areas:

- working practices may need updating
- there may be new applications and uses for existing products
- staff skills may need improving
- customer response times could be shortened

- customers may demand something that you do not currently do or supply
- new markets may be available
- customer care programmes may need to be improved
- production machinery and equipment may need to be replaced
- new products may be possible
- new technology may produce improvements
- costs could be reduced.

These – and probably several other areas – should be reviewed to see where improvements, innovations and updates will help the organisation towards its objectives. The first move is to take a careful look at the current situation.

Identifying weaknesses and strengths in the current situation

The ideal way to start assessing where changes are needed is to conduct a SWOT analysis – a list of strengths, weaknesses, opportunities and threats. The consideration of all aspects of the business that is required when preparing an analysis of this type can be very beneficial in kick-starting a process of innovation and improvement. It gives managers an opportunity to sit down and assess just what is going right and what is going wrong. This is an opportunity that all managers should make the time for, as it is too easy to keep working on the business, doing a job, possibly doing some 'fire fighting', but not really thinking deeply about the business or making the time to see if anything could be done better. With a lack of drive towards change comes stagnation and, as we discussed in Chapter 2, the consequences of staying as you are can be disastrous for a business. So, let's look at how to conduct a SWOT analysis.

A variety of sources of information should be used to compile this list of strengths, weaknesses, opportunities and threats. These include customer surveys, staff opinions and comments, market reports and analysis of competitors, and your own instincts. Then consider each area of the business carefully, assessing whether aspects of it could be a strength, weakness, opportunity or threat. To help with this process, let's consider what your list might look like. For example, your strengths could include:

- quick order turnaround times
- a product that is well-established in the market
- your organisation's reputation.

Weaknesses could include:

- low staff morale
- poor customer service
- manufacturing processes that need updating.

Opportunities could include:

- developing a new stream of business via the internet
- a competitor in difficulties
- investment in new plant.

Threats could include:

- reducing demand for your product
- new competitors in the market
- competitors using other technologies such as the internet to reach their customers.

Each element of this SWOT analysis should then inform your assessment of the need for change in all areas of your organisation.

Case study

A firm of accountants used a series of SWOT analyses to grow the business. Its first analysis highlighted many aspects of the business that could be improved plus a threat that was facing the firm in the form of improved software coming onto the market that had the potential to enable their smaller clients to complete their accounts without needing an accountant. The firm immediately put into place a plan to improve performance in a number of areas and they viewed the new software as an opportunity to market its services to small companies rather than as a threat. It used their extensive experience as a selling point and also the time-saving element of their services and actually increased the number of small businesses whose accounts it prepared on a regular basis.

The firm revisited this SWOT analysis 12 months later and realised that such an analysis represented a picture of the business at a point in time and that things could change even in as short a time as a few months. It also calculated that they had only tackled about 50 per cent of the issues that had been highlighted in the first analysis. The firm therefore realised the need to conduct a SWOT analysis on a regular basis and to keep careful track of how the recommendations were followed, setting timescales for the areas to be improved. Without this careful targeting and specific allocation of work it realised that it would not achieve its objectives.

There are other types of analysis, less well known than the SWOT analysis that will provide a structure to some of your research during strategic planning and business reviews including Five Forces analysis and PESTLE. Five Forces looks at the key elements governing the market in which an organisation operates. These are:

- Threat from new competitors – the more businesses that are competing in any market the more difficult it becomes to maintain market share or to increase prices.
- Threat of substitute products – if products are available in the market that are a close substitute for what an organisation is offering then it will be difficult to increase – or even maintain – prices. In this situation it is necessary to try to differentiate between products. An example of substitute products becoming available is that of email affecting the number of letters being posted.
- Bargaining power of customers – with a small number of large buyers in a market, customers will have a high bargaining power and be able to exert pressure on organisations to reduce prices.
- Intensity of competition – the degree of competitiveness in a market, in terms of price, marketing or innovativeness will affect an organisation. This competitiveness is dictated by a number of factors such as how many companies are competing in the market, costs, diversity of the market and the extent of the entry and exit barriers to the market.
- Bargaining power of suppliers – if there are a small number of suppliers and/or the product or service they are supplying is unique, then they will be able to dictate terms to their customers as the buyers will not have sufficient choice to enable them to change suppliers. This results in the supplier being easily able to maintain or even increase prices, affecting the profitability of an organisation in this sort of market.

Another type of business analysis, PESTLE, looks at the various external elements that will affect an organisation. It is formed from the initial letters of these elements:

- *Political* – this examines the extent to which a government's actions affect a market. These interventions include taxation, support for businesses, trade restrictions and political stability.
- *Economic* – the economy can have a huge impact on an organisation. This includes the effects of changes in interest rates, exchange rates, inflation levels and periods of 'boom or bust'.
- *Social* – trends in social issues can affect how an organisation is managed and the products and services it supplies. These social issues include demographics, marriage and family patterns and health. For example, an ageing population will demand products such as retirement housing or residential care, different types of holidays and perhaps less-fashionable clothing whereas if people with young families are the largest social grouping then there will be a higher demand for children's products, larger cars, education and fashionable clothing if teenagers form a large part of this group.
- *Technological* – the rate of technological change will affect productivity, how business processes are carried out and also competitiveness.
- *Legal* – this includes changes in employment law that will dictate minimum pay rates for example or changes in regulation in a market. Other legislation that can affect an organisation's profitability or ways of working includes health and safety law, consumer regulations and anti-discrimination law.
- *Environmental* – this has had a marked effect in recent years, especially the emphasis on climate change. This

can affect the way that a company operates and can increase costs by imposing obligations on the organisation to be environmentally-friendly – the demand to recycle, for example. The weather will also have an effect on many businesses such as those involved in tourism, agriculture and those supplying weather-sensitive items such as clothing, building insulation and umbrellas.

A similar analysis is also used concentrating on the first four elements – PEST – and a wider view can be taken using a form of analysis with the acronym SPECTACLES. This looks at several of the PEST areas but adds others that can further inform an analysis of an organisation's operating environment. It covers Social, Political, Economic, Cultural, Technological, Aesthetic, Customers, Legal, Environmental and Sectoral aspects.

Using the results of these analyses plus other data that you will be able to collect (more about this later in this section), it is possible to develop a strategy for the organisation and to see where changes may be necessary.

Case study

Any major investment requires comprehensive analysis of the type detailed above before it is made. A well-known case where inadequate research and analysis was carried out is that of the Millennium Dome. The intention was to provide a lasting facility suitable to celebrate the end of the second millennium and the start of the third, showcasing British life, but the project failed. The expected 30,000 visitors per day did not arrive and problems were experienced with getting visitors into and out of the area. In addition, the content of the exhibitions inside the Dome was not always up to the expected standard. *(Continued)*

(Continued)

So, what went wrong? There were several problems experienced that were the result of a lack of detailed analysis prior to the planning and opening of the Dome:

- It was assumed that visitors would come in large numbers regardless of the quality of the displays. This may have been true many years ago, but with new technology and the standards being applied in other exhibition areas, today's consumers will not ignore poor quality.
- Political uncertainty and doubt about who was responsible for different areas emerged.
- The location was not ideal. The Dome was situated outside of Central London, a long distance from other major attractions.
- The transport infrastructure was inadequate and severe problems getting people to the Dome and back out of the area were experienced.

Had a comprehensive analysis of all aspects of the environment in which the Dome was being built been carried out, most of the problems experienced could have been resolved. It is also possible that if such an analysis had been conducted, the Dome project might not have gone ahead in the way that it did. However, there was pressure on costs and on time, as there was an obvious deadline for opening, plus severe political pressure because this was a government-led venture. All these factors meant the project went ahead with results that became obvious and public, perfectly demonstrating the need for full evaluation of all aspects of a project before deciding to go ahead.

Check where you are now

In addition to doing one or more of the different analyses of the organisation's business and operating environment, as outlined in the previous section, you will need to answer lots of questions if you are to reach a point where you know what your current position is and what changes can produce real benefits. This research will probably involve a customer and market analysis, assessing the needs of customers and how well the organisation is meeting those needs. It should also include a review of the products and services offered by the organisation, looking at the marketing, sales, pricing, after-sales service, design and packaging. It needs to answer the question 'Which products or services are performing well and which might need to be dropped because of poor performance?' Of course, a review of production performance will also be necessary, covering costs of major purchases, production methods and systems, machinery and staffing levels. In short, everything should be reviewed and considered for change.

Asking – and finding – answers to the right questions is a key part of the change process. This phrase from Kipling's poem might help:

> 'I keep six honest serving men, they taught me all I knew, their names are What and Why and When and How and Where and Who.'

In other words, simply question everything. Let's work through an example situation. Suppose the area you were examining was that of productivity, try asking these questions:

- What do we produce?
- What could we do better?
- What do our customers say about it?

- Why do we do it the way we do?
- Why don't we do it differently?
- Why don't we sell in market X or market Y?
- When did we introduce this product or service?
- When will this product or service become unprofitable?
- How do we do what we do?
- How could we change it?
- How much profit do we make per item/worker/hour?
- How many do we produce?
- How has the quantity we produce changed over time?
- Where do we produce our goods and services – and could we produce them elsewhere?
- Where is our most profitable area?
- Who is our most profitable worker – and why?
- Who will pay more for our products or services?
- Who is our least profitable customer?
- Who is our most profitable customer?

From these few example questions the idea is clear – find out everything, don't take anything for granted, get all the data you can and find reasons for all assumptions. Only then can you decide where you are now.

A full review of business performance is a necessary prerequisite to any change process. A wide-ranging business review should be a regular part of any organisation's strategy but it could also be triggered by a variety of circumstances, such as:

- Poor performance – if the organisation is not felt to be performing as well as it could or should.
- Revision of the business plan – if it is some time since the original business plan was prepared then a business review can be used as a precursor to preparing a new one and to making the changes in direction and so on that are identified as necessary.

- Changes in the market – if new competition enters the market in which the organisation is operating, for example, or if new products are taking away the organisation's market share then changes will become an urgent necessity and a review of products, markets and competitors is invaluable.
- Growth plans – if its senior managers are ready to move it to the next level then assessing the performance of an organisation is the best way to see where change is necessary.

A strategic review of the business will help business owners and senior managers to better understand the business, including the basis for its profitability, how it works internally and how it relates to its competitors. This review must be done as realistically and in as detached a manner as possible and this is what we will look at in the next section.

Conducting a review

The aim of a business review is to get a clear picture of the organisation's current position. A full business review report should involve the following:

A summary

Include a summary of what the organisation does – this might take the form of a very brief history of the organisation, what it produces or provides to its customers, how many people are employed and so on.

Financial information

An assessment of how well the organisation is performing in financial terms – this will include financial measures such as profit, costs, cashflow, borrowings and debtor control. Are your financial controls and systems working as expected? Are future plans affordable?

Personnel

An assessment of personnel – have you got the right staff in the right jobs? Do you need more or fewer people to carry out the necessary work? What are their projected training requirements? Are people generally motivated and hard-working? Do you have a high staff turnover?

Assets review

A review of equipment, premises and working methods – this is especially important in the case of a manufacturing organisation. If machinery is old and inefficient then the business performance will not be as good as it should be. Manufacturing capability must be compared with current and projected demand.

Customer details

A thorough assessment of the customer base – including numbers, details about repeat order frequency and answers to questions such as:

- Are the customers still buying the same products and in the same quantities as when the business was last reviewed?
- Have they been asked for feedback about the organisation's customer service and, if so, was it a favourable response or are major improvements necessary in this area?

This review of customers should also include an examination of changes that may have taken place in the market in which your organisation operates.

Competition

An assessment of the organisation's competitors – there are various aspects that will need to be considered such as:

- What market share do they have compared with yours?
- How does their pricing structure compare with yours?
- Do they pay higher or lower salaries than your organisation?
- What are their staff terms and conditions?

Sales and marketing

A review of your marketing methods – take into account what is spent on sales, marketing and public relations, and how successful these parts of the business are.

Technology

Check your use of technology – it is not always necessary to use the very latest technology, but being aware of what other software systems, for example, could do for the business is essential.

- Do the programs and equipment that are currently in use still fulfil the needs of the business?
- Could improvements be achieved if the organisation invested in new technology?

At the end of such a wide-ranging review a full report on the findings is essential. This process should help to clarify where improvements may be made and will put the organisation in a position to plan changes.

Decide where you want to be

Having arrived at a complete picture of the current situation it is time now to decide what can – and should – be changed. What can change do for a business? As we discussed earlier, change is the only way to improve an organisation and all organisations must aim at continual improvement to avoid stagnation and to ensure their survival. Innovation is vital to any organisation and can be split into three broad categories in terms of what it can do and how it can be used:

1. Development of new or improved products – this is often in response to a changing marketplace or to customer demands
2. Improvement of business processes – all systems and ways of working should be continually under review so that any problems can be resolved. This will result in improved efficiency and profitability.

3. Altering of perceptions – this, in marketing terms, could refer to improving a brand's value in the marketplace or to differentiating a product or service in some way so that it becomes more competitive.

All change will be aimed at improving one of these three areas and within these three areas there will be an infinite variety of aspects that may need to change. Your task in the initial stages is deciding what to improve and how. All organisations must have a vision of where they are going, where they want to be. They must also have a strategy of how to get there. This will involve both strategic planning and then developing a business plan. The difference between these two is that strategic planning is looking at an organisation in the long term whereas writing a business plan involves setting shorter term goals and then setting out how to achieve them. Some organisations do not prepare a strategic plan, but to ignore this step is to neglect the opportunity to have an in-depth look at the business. Let's look first at how a strategic plan is developed.

Strategic planning

The first thing to realise about a strategic plan is that, being a long-term view of the organisation, it sets out the vision for the future by looking at the organisation's direction and priorities. It looks specifically at how the business can develop and grow and how it can get to where it's going. The organisation's vision, values, objectives and mission should inform the entire process of strategic planning and it is important that nothing is ruled out in the beginning. Keeping an open mind when planning the future of a business is essential so everything must be included in the review and no assumptions made about what is or is not acceptable. It may be that the financial structure of the business needs to be changed or the location of the business, for example, but many people will rule these options out without properly considering them. Looking at all the problems faced by the business and all the possible ways to grow it, and then keeping an open mind before the final strategic plan is drawn up, will help to ensure that the organisation comes up with the most effective plan for the future.

There are three main stages of strategic planning:

1. Assessing where the organisation is now – this is also known as strategic analysis.
2. Deciding where the organisation is going – this is the heart of the planning process.
3. Planning what needs to be done to get there – this takes into account resources, timescales and the implementation process.

Except in very small businesses, the strategic plan will need the input of a variety of people so that different skills and areas of knowledge are used. Often the process starts with a brainstorming session but will still require the use of large amounts of data relating to all aspects of the business including analysis of the market in which the organisation operates, its customer base and its financial situation. The final document – the strategic plan – will include:

- a market analysis
- the strengths and weaknesses of the organisation (discussed earlier in this chapter)
- a prediction about the organisation's future – where will it be in five or ten years' time, for example
- the objectives set by the owner/senior management of the organisation

- what changes will need to be made in order to achieve those objectives
- the resources needed to achieve the objectives – capital, staff, premises and so on
- where appropriate, future plans that may include acquisitions or diversification into other areas should be considered
- how the objectives will be achieved – and when.

This plan can then be used as a focus for the direction the organisation will take in the next five to ten years. Its implementation should include giving key staff 'ownership' of:

- goals – to work towards the objectives outlined in the strategic plan
- responsibilities – each area of the plan must be made the responsibility of a senior manager/owner of the business
- key performance indicators (KPIs)
- budgets – for all the resources needed to reach the objectives
- deadlines – throughout the life of the plan there should be milestones set that will signal whether or not targets are being met and indicating whether or not the plan will be delivered on time.

As always, to ensure success, all deadlines, goals and objectives should be carefully monitored and regular review dates set. The strategic plan should be kept in mind when considering any major changes and when formulating the business plan, which we will look at next.

INSTANT TIP

When the strategic plan has been written, don't keep it a secret or confine its distribution to senior management. Give every employee a copy – or at least a summary or highlights. It will give even the most junior employee an understanding of where the organisation is going and how they are going to get there, acting as a motivator as it will make the workforce feel involved.

Preparing a business plan

In contrast to the strategic plan, a business plan focuses on the short-term future of the organisation and goes into more detail about operational considerations. Its purpose is different in that whereas a strategic plan sets a direction for the organisation, the business plan clarifies how and when the organisation is going to achieve its aims, keeping in mind the vision of the organisation's long-term future and values as detailed in the strategic plan. A good business plan is vital for businesses, both new and established, as it shows how the business will develop. It will usually include the following.

An overview

An overview of the plan not only sets out the main points about the business but also summarises the rest of the business plan. This section is particularly important if the document is to be used in an effort to obtain funding for the business (for example, in the case of a start-up) as many banks and investors will make a quick decision on whether to look further into the business based on how convincing this overview is. It's a bit like the first paragraph in a novel – the reader will decide at this point whether to read on or not, so it's essential to make it interesting.

What you do

This is an overview of the business and sets out how you do what you do, i.e. the purpose of the organisation, details of its market sector, a description of its products or services and the vision for the future. Its aim can be two-fold – to attract the attention of investors and/or to focus on the vision for the business. It should detail what makes the product or service that the organisation offers different and saleable and plans of how the business will develop. As when writing anything, it is important to remember who the document is aimed at. If it is for internal use only then it can use jargon so long as it informs the senior management where the organisation is going. However, if it is intended to be used to gain financing and for external use then steer clear of jargon so that someone who doesn't know about the business in detail or its market sector will be able to understand and make judgements based on the information given.

Financial details

Business plans always include financial forecasts and these are especially important if the plan is to be used to obtain funding from a bank or other potential investor. This will cover full income and expenditure details, profit predictions, cashflow forecasts, details of assets and liabilities, sales forecasts and the funding required, plus plans for repayment and the security that may be offered for loans. This section is a way of describing the business from a financial point of view so it should mirror, using numbers, what has been said in the rest of the plan. For example, if a best-selling product has been mentioned then this section should give details of how much of this product has been sold, what the profit margin was and so on.

This section should include brief financial forecasts that cover a period of up to five years, while including detailed information about the first year.

How you do the work

This should cover areas such as what manufacturing equipment is used, the use of IT and what systems are in place to monitor the activities of the organisation (management accounting, performance improvement plans and so on). It should also include details of where the operations are carried out and answer questions relating to who owns the premises and the advantages and disadvantages of the current premises, plus any plans to develop the site or to relocate.

Details of plans to outsource any work should be included here and a summary of the facilities available.

People

This section should answer the question 'Who will do the work?' Starting with the total number of people employed by the organisation, this section should go on to detail the skills and strengths of the workforce and how any gaps in the skills will be filled where necessary, perhaps with training and/or recruitment.

Next it should look at who will manage the work. Details of the management team responsible for leading the organisation should be included here. This can be an important factor when looking for funding, so it is essential to 'sell' the expertise of the management team by including details of their qualifications and experience, and explaining how the blend of skills in the team helps the business.

Your market

Here you will concentrate on your sales targets and how you will achieve them. This should include details of the organisation's customer base and its competitors. A description of the organisation's products and their place in the market is invaluable here, as are details of how they will be marketed and priced. There should be plenty of information of how the products will be promoted and how the selling operation works. How you get the products to market must be explained – do you use agents, or sell online for example?

This section should include sufficient detail about pricing, competition, marketing, sales forecasts and how the predicted results will be achieved to show that the organisation has a thorough understanding of the market in which it operates or plans to operate. Finally, it needs to show in sufficient detail that the sales targets are realistic and achievable.

Risk management

Include details of the risks to the organisation in this section. This is an assessment of the risks that the organisation will face in the short term and can include a variety of risks such as fire or other disaster, loss of main personnel, competitor activity and equipment failure plus the insurance cover taken out and the actions planned to deal with these risks.

INSTANT TIP

If you're preparing a business plan to help you to obtain initial funding from a bank, make sure that you present it well – put it in a professional-looking binder, double-check it for errors – and keep it short. A scruffy document that's over-long will not make the right impression for your new business.

Using your strategic and business plans

When you've finished your strategic planning and have prepared your business plan, don't just file them away. They are meant to be used. Your strategic plan will help to keep the vision and values of the organisation at the front of your mind so that everything that you do helps to work towards your vision and complies with your values. Your business plan should be consulted regularly as a working document. It will help to focus your efforts in developing the business and ensure that what you are doing will move you in the right direction. Implementation of both the strategic and the business plans must be carefully monitored. The business plan, in particular, should include deadlines showing when important aspects of the plan are to be achieved and responsibilities should be assigned to each area.

If the business plan is not being used for the purpose of securing finance, then there may be several other advantages and changes that the review which is necessary in order to prepare a comprehensive business plan will bring. Examples of the changes and revelations that can come about when a thorough review of an organisation's methods, results and current situation is undertaken include:

- a realisation that technology needs to be updated
- supply contracts may need to be renegotiated
- a change of direction is overdue
- a realisation that the direction that was originally planned for the business has not been followed. (This can be good – if the new direction is the one that everyone agrees must be followed – or bad – if the new direction had been followed by accident and has not produced advantages for the organisation. If the new direction is not desirable then this will be an opportunity to get the organisation back on track.)
- training needs may be highlighted
- information about aspects of the organisation that is shown up by the review may prove unexpectedly useful and allow managers and staff to concentrate on areas that need attention.

Reviewing the plans

Finally, it is essential to review both the business plan and the strategic plan on a regular basis. Not only will this demonstrate to you how things change over months and years but will also help to keep you on track. The plans that were right for the organisation perhaps a year ago are not necessarily the right plans now. They will certainly not remain the right plans indefinitely. A regular update of both these important documents are a perfect opportunity to take stock of your business and perhaps change things to ensure you reach your goals.

Many organisations find it difficult, even after preparing a business plan that shows them precisely where they are right now, to see where they should go. In this case it can be useful to enlist outside help. A consultant or other business adviser may be better able to stand back and assess what needs to be done and to set a broad direction for the future of the organisation in conjunction with its stakeholders. The options in this situation include:

- Employing a suitable business consultant to install new systems – here it is essential to find someone who has experience in dealing with the types of problem you are experiencing.
- Taking the advice of a business consultant on matters such as structure, systems, purchasing, IT and so on.
- Appointing a non-executive director – again, appropriate experience is necessary. Non-executive directors are often appointed on a one or two days per month basis to advise and give an impartial assessment of an organisation's situation and performance. Sometimes a director of this type will be used to bring prestige to an organisation if they are well-known and respected in a particular field.

Employing business consultants can be an expensive option but many contracts specify payment per day's work and are also linked to results achieved. Contracts with consultants need to be drawn up very carefully. Your local Business Link or Chamber of Commerce can often recommend suitable consultants and advise on how an organisation can employ them.

Benefits of innovation

A simple definition of innovation is 'creating value from ideas'. If an organisation genuinely has innovation as a value then this will lead to it doing things better. It may be useful at this point to look at the difference between creativity and innovation. Creativity usually refers to doing something new that has not been done before whereas innovation refers to a change to an existing process or product. The latter can involve introducing new products and services or improvements to existing ones. It can also mean changes to existing work methods and systems.

So, what are the benefits of innovation? They can be many and varied depending on the type of change introduced, but include:

- increased efficiency
- increased profitability
- greater competitiveness
- better use of resources
- improved productivity
- reduced costs
- more employee involvement
- greater responsiveness to customer requirements
- increased customer satisfaction
- reduced waste
- improved product design.

Obviously, all organisations will need to achieve at least some of the benefits listed above and for innovation to take place ideas are required, so developing a culture of innovation in an organisation is essential. There will be more about this in the next chapter.

Identifying opportunities

In the initial stages of assessing where change is needed that would be advantageous to the organisation, it is useful to concentrate on the three areas for innovation:

1. *Development of new or improved products*. As we discussed previously, all products and services have a lifecycle so that eventually each product will come to a point when it will not give an organisation the profit it needs and will have to be replaced. An ongoing review of the sales of each product line will show you which ones are in decline and which therefore need to be replaced. You may also get indications from customers – maybe from a customer survey you have carried out – that new or improved products are required. Your marketing department, research and development department or any teams or processes you have set up to encourage innovation may also come up with a completely new product that will complement your existing product range. They may also suggest ways in which products can be improved or altered slightly to fill a gap in the market.

2. *Improvement of business processes*. This covers an extremely wide area of possible change. For example, it could involve an overhaul of your buying process in an effort to make it more efficient and to reduce costs by sourcing other suppliers or changing the grade of product purchased. Alternatively it could involve the distribution process, various areas of manufacturing, administrative processes and so on.

3. *Altering perceptions*. Changes in this area will usually be driven by marketing. It may be that the direction of your marketing efforts is changed. For example, it may be decided that your products are perceived in the marketplace as less reliable than those of your competitors. In this case, the marketing people may be able to change the emphasis of the advertising and marketing literature that they distribute so that it reflects a different view of the product, concentrating perhaps less on price or availability and more on reliability.

The main focus when identifying opportunities for change is to be aware of what is happening in your organisation, your marketplace and in similar organisations. Research and work in these areas will pay dividends in terms of possible improvements. This research should cover what developments your competitors are planning or have recently introduced, what your customers want and how effective your current business processes are.

An important source of ideas for innovation is, of course, the workforce. There are two reasons why staff should be included in the ideas-forming process:

1. Employees are a valuable source of knowledge about the organisation, its competitors and the market it has to compete in.
2. If they are included in this process they are far more likely to cooperate with change when it happens as they will then have 'ownership' of the ideas.

So, having seen that it will be beneficial to all concerned to get ideas for innovation from the workforce, how can you facilitate this process? A variety of methods can be used to involve staff in generating ideas including suggestion boxes and schemes, rewards and so on (see Chapter 4). An effective way of generating ideas is to hold brainstorming meetings. This is when you hold a team meeting – but not too many attendees as it's essential for everyone to have input so make the meetings specific to small teams and departments – with the simple objective of getting as many ideas on the table as possible. There should be no attempt at this point to evaluate the ideas in any way. Follow these steps to ensure a productive brainstorming session:

- Set a time limit – a lot of ideas can be produced in a relatively short time so do not allow this session to run on indefinitely.

- Inform everyone of the purpose of the meeting and that no judgements are to be made at this stage.
- Reassure everyone that there will not be any criticism of whatever ideas they come up with.
- Encourage everyone to take a 'what if?' approach to the generation of ideas.
- Give them a bit of thinking time – supply everyone with a pen and paper and tell them they have ten minutes to think of ideas before the session commences.
- Choose a method of contributing ideas – either everyone taking turns or the less organised method of simply shouting out ideas as they come to people. Taking turns is obviously easier to control and will ensure that even the less pushy members of the team have a chance to put their ideas on the table but needs one rule – only one idea per turn. (If someone is unable to come up with an idea when it is their turn, move swiftly on to avoid embarrassment.)
- Record the ideas on a flipchart or whiteboard so that everyone can see them – this not only lets people see their own ideas up on the board but also acts as a catalyst for other ideas. It is important that no editing, censorship or judging goes on in the process of recording the ideas – simply record the idea as it was put to the session and move on to the next contributor.
- Limit everyone's input to briefly stating their idea. At this stage you do not want long, rambling explanations of how it would work – just the basic idea.

At the end of this process you should have a selection of ideas to study. Certainly, you should have more ideas than you could possibly act upon. The challenge now is to sift through these and end up with just a few that you will be able to take forward. The following should help to reduce the list.

Eliminate ideas that will not work

Get rid of the obvious non-starters – go through the list with the team who attended the brainstorming session and eliminate those ideas that they think just will not work. You will find that discarding some ideas will get immediate agreement from the team. Don't worry about how many 'useless' ideas you have to throw away as this just shows how successful the brainstorming process was.

Clarify

Ask the team if any ideas still on the list require clarification – at this stage you should be aiming to make things less vague but not to hold a discussion on the advantages or disadvantages of the idea.

Group similar ideas together

A brief assessment will probably reveal that some ideas left on the list are duplicated or have an obvious link, and you will be able to discard more ideas at this point.

Evaluate the ideas

Here you can start to discuss the merits of the individual ideas that you have left. Remember that exactly who had the idea is irrelevant at this stage. The person chairing the meeting should lead this discussion by asking questions such as 'What will this improve, and how?', 'What resources will be needed?' and 'Do you think this will work?'

After this meeting you should be left with a workable number of ideas plus valuable feedback from your team and this can all be taken forward to the next stage – developing a business case for change, which we will look at in the next section.

Developing a business case for change

Innovation and change must be closely allied to the strategic plans for the organisation. If the senior managers or owners of the organisation are continually reviewing both their business and what is happening in the market sector in which it operates, then the key areas for moving forward will already be known. It is vital to concentrate on the ideas in these areas first. (See earlier in this chapter for more information about strategic planning.) In developing a business case for any particular change, all the ideas should be assessed by looking at the potential for profit or savings in them one by one. This can be done by:

- Knowing the market – as we said, what is happening in your sector is a vital element in business planning for change.
- Knowing the competition – who are they and what are they doing now? How has their direction changed recently? If they are moving towards a niche market approach, for example, how does this affect your organisation? Will you compete in a similar area or go for a mass market approach?
- Knowing your customers – an analysis of your customer base is an essential part of any business case development. Combining what is evident from the orders they place with what they tell you about what they want, and about the market and your competitors will give you

vital information about where your organisation should be heading.
● Knowing your suppliers – companies who supply you with raw materials, components or simply office supplies will almost always have a wealth of information about other businesses in your area and in your business sector.

With all this information it will be possible to decide which specific ideas for change to pursue. The next step is to use the information to see how the changes will affect the organisation. Even minor changes can have a knock-on effect on many things so you should consider:

● What resources may be needed?
● Where will the money come from? Will you need to obtain a loan? If so, what will the cost be and for how long will the loan be required?
● Will extra training be required?
● How will changes affect the way you currently work? Will you have to change sales methods, for example? Or will you need to produce new sales literature, marketing plans and so on?
● Will you need more staff – or will you need to reduce your workforce?
● Will any changes to your business premises be required?
● Will you need to enlist any external help?

Finally, it will be necessary to incorporate all the answers to these questions into a business case by setting out a new business plan that includes the changes and the effect of those changes. This should include:

● setting new goals and objectives
● plans for how you will achieve those goals

- the effect on the organisation – its staff, premises, business practices, etc.
- the resources required
- a new budget – how much will the changes cost and what will be the effect on profitability?

Setting this sort of plan down in writing is a great help in seeing the changes and their effects more clearly and will form a sound basis of a business case for change.

Case study

Even what is probably the best known retailer on the British high street – Marks & Spencer – can make mistakes when trying to innovate. At the end of the twentieth century M&S decided to enter the youth fashion market. It assessed the size of the market and decided that there was capacity for a new entrant and that M&S had spare capacity for the new range in its stores. However, M&S did not research the new market sufficiently well and the launch was a failure, causing decreased sales in a number of ways:

- Sales of existing, core products that had previously been successful declined. This was because the company's marketing efforts were concentrated on the new, younger market rather than its established ranges.
- Its target market perceived M&S stores as staid, boring and not somewhere they would like to shop or where they would be likely to find something that suited them.
- Older customers – the company's core market – felt they were being ignored and visited the stores less often, ultimately finding their requirements elsewhere.

This shows that although a newer, more lucrative market may be shown to exist, success is not guaranteed and the necessary research into current and possible customer bases must be done very thoroughly, rather than making assumptions, to avoid mistakes of this type. Assumptions (such as assuming that because the market exists it will buy from you) and preconceptions (such as the ideas that younger people had about M&S) are waiting to trip up even the most experienced.

Restructuring a business

A major change that a business may go through is that of restructuring. Sometimes an organisation needs to be structured differently. This may be when the business is starting to become established and it has outgrown its original set-up or it may be when external changes prompt a major review and it becomes obvious that a different way of organising how the business is run is necessary.

In the case of a developing organisation, it is likely that when it was first set up there was a limited number of employees, the overheads were deliberately kept low and the goals were limited. The business owner would maybe have concentrated on getting the business off the ground rather than planning for the long term. However, a short while down the line, when the business has achieved its initial aims and is going well, it may become apparent that fundamental changes are needed to grow it further. This may occur when:

● Growth is impossible with the current management structure.

- New skills – such as in accountancy, marketing or production – need to be brought in. (These may be functions taken on initially by the owner but which must be carried out at a higher skills level in order to improve the way business is carried out.)
- The workload becomes impossible to manage with current staffing levels.
- Additional financing may be required.

Things that happen outside an organisation may also trigger a restructuring. These events include:

- Demand for the organisation's products or services changes.
- New technology presents different solutions to problems.
- Competitors launch new product ranges.
- New competitors enter the market.
- New markets for the organisation's products open up.

If any of these external factors makes it impossible to achieve the organisation's objectives with its current structure then it may be necessary to reorganise how the business is run. In the case of new product ranges being launched by competitors, for example, it may be necessary to restructure the organisation by setting up a separate marketing department to develop and launch new products for the organisation where previously the limited marketing that had been done was carried out by people in the sales department. Another major reason for restructuring an organisation may be when a business is taken over or merges with another one and reorganising and reconciling two different structures and cultures will be necessary.

The key thing to remember with any of these reasons for restructuring is that they should be carried out sooner rather than later. If the organisation is in deep trouble because of changes in the market or if the person who started the business waits until they are physically and mentally exhausted before making changes and getting help, then it will be more difficult to take a logical and measured approach to the changes.

There are a number of ways in which businesses can be structured.

By product group

If an organisation produces or supplies a number of distinct products or services it may be possible to group these together into departments, each of which services a different product group. In effect, each of these departments would then become a small business with all the different skills and functions being present in each one. This can be advantageous in that each department is autonomous and responsible for producing its own results and achieving its own objectives. This way of structuring an organisation will lead to a clearer focus on a product's success and on the market in which it is sold and has to compete. Where there are clear product divisions, with each of the product groups having its own customers, customer satisfaction will usually be higher with this type of restructuring as customers will be able to speak with sales people who have specialist product knowledge. However, if there is a lot of overlap of customers between the different product groups, this can become unwieldy for customers as they may have to speak to several sales departments within one organisation.

This type of structure can however be disadvantageous in that functions such as sales or accounts may be duplicated several times within the organisation. A compromise way of structuring the business may be possible, with each product's department handling most of the work and decisions for its own product area but using a centralised accounts department, for example.

By geographical area

Larger organisations such as multi-national companies or retail chains may find it appropriate to structure the business by geographical area. So, for example, a transport forwarding company could have a division handling Northern Europe, another dealing with Southern Europe, one handling the UK and one servicing the rest of the world, with specialist knowledge and experience coming into play in each of the divisions and with them being located according to their geographical area of responsibility. Again, some functions could be split according to these areas and other functions, such as human resources or accounting, looked after from a central services section of the organisation. This type of structure can work well where local knowledge is required but can result in duplication of work roles. Also, extra care will have to be taken to ensure that all the departments work towards goals agreed for the entire organisation.

By function

A very common way of structuring an organisation is by the function or role carried out by the different departments. This is more prevalent in larger companies where there are sufficient staff numbers to form departments according to function – for example, accounts, sales and production departments with individual workers and managers in each of the different departments with their own responsibilities relating to the work of that function.

The advantages of this type of structure are that there are clear lines of responsibility and, with specialisation, each member of staff will become more experienced in their role and will have a clear understanding of what is required.

As always, there are disadvantages. These include departments becoming insular and self-protecting, resulting in a resistance to change and a lack of sharing of ideas. It can also lead to competition between departments that may eventually cause problems. Often department heads in this type of structure will start to compete with each other when presenting results or when trying to gain resources for their own departments. This can lead to bad feeling and to the needs of the organisation as a whole being ignored, as department heads and their staff will naturally focus on the needs of their own departments. In this sort of structure, extra effort will have to be made to ensure that the workforce does not become resistant to change and also to integrate the different departments so that an organisation-wide culture is created rather than each department having its own culture and directions.

By specific projects

Although it is possible to work with an organisational structure arranged according to projects – especially where the organisation handles large projects that last for many years, for example, a construction company working on large public projects – it is more common for this type of structure to be used as a temporary arrangement alongside a structure arranged by function. In this case, a project team may be set up to complete a specific project such as developing a new product or changing an IT system, with members from the various departments of the organisation being, in effect, seconded to the project. On completion of the project the team will be disbanded and its members will return to their original departments and roles. This way of working can be very successful as not only does it ensure that teams are allowed to concentrate on specific, important projects with clear goals and objectives, but the structure also gives members of the team the opportunity to gain experience of working in different ways and with different people. It can help to foster an attitude of cooperation within the organisation and ensure that good ideas and ways of working are not kept within departments but are shared across the organisation. It is, however, essential that responsibilities and reporting structures are clearly defined to avoid confusion for the people that are seconded.

Major restructurings of whatever type should never be carried out in a hurry or without first carrying out the necessary research and a thorough review of the organisation (there was more about this earlier in this chapter). In addition to this research, it will be useful to prepare a chart of the existing structure – showing lines of responsibility, work flows and how the existing processes work – and then to prepare a new chart showing the same things but for the proposed structure. The main priority should be to ensure that the structure of the organisation works well to achieve the aims and objectives of the business as a whole.

SUMMARY

In this chapter we addressed the question 'When is change needed?' and found that, as improvements are always needed in business, the answer is 'always'. The first step should be to check the current position and a SWOT analysis (Strengths, Weaknesses, Opportunities and Threats) is a very useful way of doing this along with a complete review of the business and the business strategy. Alternative types of analysis were briefly examined.

The next step is to decide where the organisation needs to be. Improvements will be in one of three areas – developing new or improved products in response to market forces, improving business processes to ensure that things are done more efficiently or effectively, or altering perceptions, perhaps by improving a brand's value.

We then went on to define innovation (the creating of value from ideas) and to look at the benefits of innovation, which include increased efficiency and profitability. Brainstorming sessions will yield plenty of initial ideas for innovation and these can be evaluated to reduce them to a manageable number. A business case for change can then be made by evaluating the effect of the proposed changes on the business using knowledge about the organisation's customers, suppliers, competitors and market.

Finally, we looked at restructuring and the ways in which an organisation can be structured.

ACTION CHECKLIST

1. Conduct a brief SWOT analysis of your organisation.
2. Which of the three areas that can be improved by a change programme – i.e. developing new or improved products, doing things better by improving business processes or altering perceptions – do you think would most benefit your organisation?
3. Have a brainstorming session of your own to generate ideas for innovation in your organisation or department. Give yourself a time limit of just 15 minutes and let your mind wander, using a 'what if' approach rather than restricting your thoughts to tried and tested paths.
4. Using your knowledge of your business or department, consider which of the ideas generated are viable and what effect they would have on the business if implemented.
5. How is your organisation structured? Do you think it would be as effective if structured differently?

04

Where will you get ideas for change and innovation?

For any innovation to happen a supply of ideas is needed. These ideas can come from both inside and outside the business. The internally generated ones will come mainly from employees and may arise in the normal course of work or from specially targeted programmes aimed at generating ideas in specific areas. Ideas may also be generated within the organisation by way of research programmes. Ideas from outside the organisation may result from customer surveys, supplier contacts, market research and general market forces such as new technology or products becoming available. In order to avoid stagnation and falling profitability in an organisation, ideas must continually be generated, assessed and exploited. In this chapter we will concentrate on how those ideas can be generated and also look at how the initial assessment of the viability of ideas can be carried out.

Developing an organisational strategy for innovation

Generating the ideas is the first stage towards benefiting from change in any organisation. As we saw above, ideas can come from both internal and external sources. It is important to create the right environment so that ideas are routinely put forward within an organisation. To get everyone in an organisation in a position to be able to contribute to this creative process, the systems, structures and attitudes must be in place. These include the following.

Encourage the right atmosphere

There should be openness between all employees and between different departments so that workers are not embarrassed to put forward their ideas or constrained by bureaucratic systems. This can be done by encouraging interaction between departments. One good way of doing this is to set up joint projects with teams formed from different departments.

Get the message out

Senior managers must make it clear that they will support innovation and will look seriously at any ideas put forward and then make the necessary resources available to put viable ideas into action. Everyone should be aware of management's attitude to innovation. They should know that there is commitment from the top and that this will be backed with action and resources rather than management merely paying lip service to continual improvement.

Spread the responsibility

It must be made clear that innovation will improve the business so it is for everyone's benefit and is therefore everyone's responsibility.

Don't penalise risk

Nothing was ever gained without some element of risk so it is important that people know they will not be punished if they take a chance on an idea (so long as it has been properly assessed) and it does not work out as hoped. It is essential that people feel that they will be supported if they come up with the right idea rather than criticised. To come up with ideas for improvement people must be interested in, and committed to, their jobs and the organisation so this is a situation that should be encouraged rather than discouraged.

Generate enthusiasm

This must come from the top. Senior management must show their commitment to change and improvement. Publicising the success of previous changes, perhaps by company newsletters or the organisation's website, can encourage this.

Use suggestion boxes

Put these in communal areas to encourage people to use them and make it known that the contents of suggestion boxes will be taken seriously. Publicise the system of reviewing suggestions and of putting viable suggestions into action.

Hold workshops or regular meetings

Use these to brainstorm ideas. These should be within working teams as well as getting teams from different departments together so that there is some 'cross-pollination' of ideas.

Set up lines of communication

Things such as newsletters, suggestion boxes, innovation schemes and team meetings can be used to ensure that people with ideas can make them known. It is important that if a team member in one department has an idea, they do not keep it to themselves if there is a chance that it would be beneficial to another department. The easier it is to get an idea out there, the more likely people will be to take part in the process of innovation.

Recruit the right people

Look specifically for people with ideas and creativity when recruiting for any position. Make this a particular focus of interviews.

Reward good ideas

If ideas work and produce benefits for the organisation then the person or team responsible for generating the idea should receive a suitable incentive. There will be more about incentive schemes in Chapter 7.

Celebrate success

When it works, let everyone know. Hold a small party, announce it in the newsletter and on the website, and inform the local or trade press. This has two-fold benefits – the person or team who came up with the idea feels rewarded and it also publicises the attitude to change that is held in the organisation.

INSTANT TIP

Make sure that senior people are heavily involved in idea generation – don't just leave it to junior staff. This not only makes everyone aware of the importance of innovation but also senior managers will be able to overcome the inevitable obstacles that will present themselves in the initial stages.

Developing initial ideas

Workshops to take suggestions from the ideas stage to something more workable are a good idea. They must include a selection of people from different disciplines so that how the idea might work can be developed from start to finish. It is important to remember that change will only work if plenty of attention is given to the 'people aspect' of the idea. This must be given as much attention as the technological or production details. Sometimes, organisations will plan production changes in minute detail and almost ignore the people involved in the change. They may throw in a bit of training on a new piece of machinery but not consider how new shift patterns may help the change or how workers may be worried that productivity gains may lead to job losses.

A successful workshop at the beginning of a change process will consider the implications of the change from start to finish. A checklist of items to take into account at this stage would include answers to the following:

- What will the gains be?
- What might we lose?
- Who will be directly affected by this?
- Who will be indirectly affected by this?
- How do they feel about this?
- How much training will be needed – and who needs it?
- How will work patterns or methods be affected?
- Will we need new job descriptions?
- Do we have the staff to cope with this change?
- What new resources will be required?
- What could go wrong?
- How long will the change process take?
- Have we done all the necessary research?
- How will customers be affected?

The aim at this initial development stage should be to analyse each suggestion that has made it through the selection process and find answers to each of the above questions. The ideas can then be further whittled down until what is left is one or two viable ideas for change that the organisation can take forward. The answers to these questions will not only help in the selection and development of ideas at the initial stage but will also inform the detailed planning that must go on before any changes can be made.

Spotting and encouraging creativity

The people who will be of most help to you in challenging the status quo and coming up with innovative ideas that will bring change to the organisation are not those who are simply happy in their work and comfortable where they are. Those people may be among your best workers but they will not be your best innovators. You need to look for the passionate, driven people in your organisation. They may perhaps be viewed in the organisation as rebels or awkward people who do not conform to the respectful, accepting stereotype of a 'good worker'. They will be noticeably willing to take risks. If you've got one or two – or more – of these people then put them to work on being creative.

Set them a challenge to improve one area of the business and leave them alone to come up with ideas. Obviously, you cannot just hand over responsibility for change to these dissatisfied people but they will be almost certain to come up with ideas quickly and may already have formulated plans to improve their own work area. These ideas must be given serious consideration. Having asked them to come up with ideas and plans, management cannot simply dismiss them and force through their own ideas. If it is found that their plans are unrealistic and unworkable then management must come up with solid reasons as to why they will not work and why they cannot be implemented. If suitable consideration is not given to their ideas, there is a risk of demotivating or even losing some of these valuable employees.

Key stages of innovation

There are several stages that an organisation must go through in order to become more innovative and to bring about change where it has been judged necessary and viable. These are as follows:

Set a strategy

This involves deciding what the organisation wants to achieve and making innovation a priority. Continuous improvement must become part of the strategy for the organisation.

Change the culture if necessary

This may involve changing the attitudes and beliefs that are held within the organisation and overcoming many barriers. It will not be something that will happen in the short term and will need a multi-angled approach over a sustained period. This approach will have to include making change part of the strategy of the organisation, as noted above, and also making this known both inside and outside the organisation. Improvement must become part of everything that the organisation does.

Develop initial ideas

Get the ideas out on the table from all the different sources – staff, customers, the market, stakeholders and suppliers – and then examine them carefully to see if they are viable and will take the organisation in its planned direction.

Set goals and objectives

Any change must have targets to aim at and these should involve what you want to achieve and when you want to achieve it. Milestones along the way so that you can check progress are extremely useful. It is important that, having set these targets, they are made clear to everyone involved.

Plan the change

It is best to produce a formal document that details the planned change. This should be easy to understand and include the necessary commitment for the change and specify who is leading the change. Goals should be made clear and it needs to include a breakdown of the work required and necessary resources to achieve the change.

Select a team

Prior to the start of any change programme ensure not only that there are sufficient numbers of people to carry out the planned work but also that the team possesses the necessary variety of skills and work styles. In selecting the team, consideration should also be given to personalities, capabilities and strengths.

Arrange resources

This includes items such as finances, time and extra expertise or training that may be required. At the same time, consider how the resources are to be controlled and who will take responsibility for this important aspect of change management.

Implement the change

Announce the start date of the change programme and make sure that this is adhered to. If the planning has been done properly, everyone on the change team will know what their responsibilities are.

There are also several well-recognised systems that can help to implement major change programmes. These include Total Quality Management (TQM), Business Process Re-engineering (BPR) and Six Sigma – more about these in Chapter 5.

Monitor the change

Regular assessments of how the change process is going and the results that are being achieved are essential. The results of such evaluations must be used to update, refocus and redirect the change process whenever necessary. If unexpected obstacles have been found that may derail or delay the change process then they must be dealt with.

There will be more details about these aspects of implementation in the following chapters.

SUMMARY

In this chapter we went into more detail about innovation including how to get the initial ideas. This involves having an organisational strategy for innovation and creating the right environment for change. This uses a variety of methods including regular meetings and brainstorming sessions, suggestion boxes, improved communication to make everyone aware of the need for innovation, rewarding and celebrating successes, and recruiting and developing the right people. This will ensure that creativity is identified and encouraged.

We then looked at the key stages of innovation from setting an organisation-wide strategy, changing the culture where necessary and setting goals and objectives, to the processes of planning, implementation and monitoring the changes.

ACTION CHECKLIST

1. How many of the suggested ways of creating the right environment for change does your own organisation use?
2. Assess your organisation with reference to how it encourages change and innovation.
3. Assess your own attitude to change – are you a creative person?
4. Consider the last change that you and your organisation implemented. Did you go through all the stages mentioned above? If not, why not? Was the change successful?
5. What were the goals and objectives of a successful change process that you have recently taken part in? Consider how they were set.

05

How can you introduce change?

Key management challenges of developing ideas

Generating ideas is a challenge but, having come up with some suitable ideas that will improve performance in an organisation, there are even greater challenges ahead. Many organisations have a long, unwieldy process for developing and assessing ideas and they apply it to all change projects, large and small. A more flexible approach will get smaller change projects producing results far more quickly and easily. For smaller projects, having decided that an idea has potential and that it does not require significant resources, then every effort should be made to get the change into operation as quickly as possible.

Obviously, if a major change is under consideration then it will require huge amounts of time, money and effort to push through and will have far-reaching consequences for the organisation. In this case, every effort must be made to examine the project from every angle before putting the change process into action.

The challenges facing an organisation planning a change programme are the issues that we will deal with in this chapter. But first, let's look briefly at the steps in the thinking that should be behind any change, large or small:

1. What is being changed? Look at the how, when, where, why, what.
2. Check the feasibility, taking into account the organisation and the market in which it operates.
3. Review and manage the risks.

Now, we'll move on to assessing change and the necessary resources.

Reviewing resources needed for innovation and change

A variety of resources will be needed for any substantial change programme. Although money is obviously a major consideration in whether many change programmes can go ahead, this is far from the only type of resource that is vital for success. The resources needed will usually include the following.

Capital

As we said, money is often a major consideration at the planning stage of change programmes. Arrangements may have to be made to be sure that the necessary finance will be available when required. If considerable expenditure is planned for a change programme then it will be necessary to ensure that the capital is available before giving the go ahead. It may be available for a limited time only and this may affect the timing and duration of the project.

Time

It is management's responsibility to ensure that the staff involved in making change happen have sufficient time to do it. This can be one of the most difficult aspects of change as most people are too busy doing their everyday jobs to take on – and complete successfully – a lot of extra work on something new. In the case of major change programmes, teams may need to be formed from existing personnel, or firms of consultants brought in to manage the change. It is also possible, of course, to hire temporary staff to cover periods when existing staff will need to leave their duties to do more work on the change programme.

Expertise

There are three options here. First, you can utilise existing staff if you are convinced that they have the necessary skills. Second, you can train existing staff in the areas where they are weak, and third you can bring in expertise from outside the organisation. Obviously, there are advantages and disadvantages to all of these options. The ideal would be for existing staff, who are familiar with the organisation and current methods, to be able to carry out all the extra duties and responsibilities connected with the change programme. However, this is very rarely the case except with small changes and a mix of the different options is often the solution, i.e. some duties carried out by existing staff, some degree of training being necessary and some extra help brought in – maybe from other departments or from temporary staff.

Bringing in external help may have both advantages and disadvantages. Any form of external help could take some time to make an impact as individuals will have to get to grips with the problems and the organisation before they are able to make any meaningful changes. However, both change consultants and temporary staff are usually very quick to start work. The nature of their work and expertise is such that they 'hit the ground running' as they will be well used to finding their way around an unfamiliar organisation. They will also have a distinct advantage in that they will come to a situation without any preconceptions or resistance to change. People working for an organisation that is to go through a major change programme may well have set ideas about how things should be done. They will often be resistant to change and not fully understand how the changes could work as well as, if not better, than the status quo. With external help this situation can often be overcome.

Technology

Is this available already or will the organisation have to invest in new technology? Who will decide what is required? Will extra staff – or fewer staff – be needed to operate it?

The acquisition and commissioning of extensive new systems – for example, new software systems to manage accounts departments or a large piece of computerised machinery to change production methods – can be a lengthy and complicated process with help needed from the manufacturers of the software or machinery. There will also be a period of time needed to become used to the new technology and additional training will often be required. Careful supervision and monitoring will be necessary to ensure that the full benefit of the change is achieved.

Commitment and enthusiasm

One final – but vital – resource must be present for the success of any change process, large or small, and that is enthusiasm. This must come from the top, as senior managers will have to show the workforce that they are completely behind any change programme that is implemented and will also have to ensure that the people who have to do the work understand the objectives. This enthusiasm must be conveyed and engendered in the workforce. They must fully understand and be enthusiastic about the process and about the advantages that will be gained.

As we discussed briefly above, one of the most important resources needed for innovation is time. Some organisations, such as Google, allocate a specific amount of time each week or month for staff to do nothing except be innovative. They are freed from the responsibilities of their usual work roles to do what is necessary to generate ideas for the organisation. This could be viewed as a risky strategy but at Google it has paid off in terms of innovative new developments (for example, Google Earth™) that have generated considerable extra revenue.

Not only is time needed for the generation of innovative ideas but also time must be allocated to teams to implement the change. It is almost inevitable that employees will have to keep their usual jobs going at the same time as putting in place a new system of working but every effort must be made to ensure that they have the time to work on something new. If no time is allowed then failure is far more likely. It would be wise to employ extra staff to do routine work in a department undergoing change or to bring in a manager who could coordinate the change process and spend the necessary time on communicating with team members. Trying to force through a change without allocating extra resources in terms of time would be a false economy; either the change will not be implemented to best effect or the everyday work of the department would suffer, resulting in losses in either case.

Removing obstacles to innovation

One of the main obstacles to innovation is inertia. Doing what you have always done is almost always easier than doing something new. But, as the saying goes, 'do what you've always done and you'll get what you've always got'. This has a lot of truth in it but the reality could be worse. As we have seen, refusing to change can result in events overtaking an organisation and the situation steadily deteriorating. At all times, in any organisation there will be a need for change but nevertheless management and staff will keep doing what they have always done, seemingly to ignore the need for change. There are many reasons for this.

Lack of leadership

Very little will change in any organisation if the people at its top or its owners do not recognise the need for change or do not know how to lead change. For an innovative culture to develop, one of the first requisites is commitment and strong leadership from the owners and/or senior management. Without this very little will change.

A satisfaction with the status quo

Many organisations are set up with a specific aim and will continue to work towards this aim without questioning whether the direction is still right or without taking into account any external changes. A business plan was probably prepared when the organisation was being set up and it may have been used to obtain a bank loan or other financing, then put away in a drawer and never seen again.

People will muddle through with perhaps only a vague idea of the organisation's strategy and with no real vision of what could be done. But an organisation that is forward thinking and recognises the need for change will continually review such plans, changing direction and business processes accordingly.

In a profitable company it is quite common for management to have the attitude of 'if it isn't broke, don't fix it'. This is acceptable only in the short term. Over the long term many things will change and a self-satisfied organisation will be caught napping. For example, the organisation's products may become obsolete and by the time management has realised this it may be too late to recover lost customers. Or it may be that new technology could ensure that cost savings are made or customer service improved to ensure that the organisation remains competitive. So many external changes can occur that could eventually lead to the demise of any organisation that is not continually searching for improvement.

Tradition

If things have always been done in a particular way, and if the workforce and/or management have been there for some time, then there may be a strong feeling that there is no need to change and that it would be breaking with tradition to do so. The pull of tradition can be very strong. Removing this obstacle can be a long and difficult task. It often requires a strong, charismatic leader who is determined to achieve improvement within the organisation.

Communication

Poor communication is also often a barrier to innovation and this can manifest itself in different ways. For example, different departments will keep themselves to themselves rather than share ideas. In this case it is essential that measures are taken to encourage cross-departmental fertilisation of ideas and working methods. This will need to be led from the top and may involve interdepartmental meetings and workshops. Insufficient communication can also lead to a lack of understanding of the need for change. Unless the workforce are given sufficient opportunity to fully understand the need for change, how this will be managed and what can be achieved, then there will be a barrier to innovation and change.

Fear

Fear will affect how change is viewed. Most people have a fear of failure so they resist trying anything new. It is, of course, almost always far easier to remain with the status quo, but things don't stay the same forever and, as we have said previously, an organisation that doesn't change of its own accord will eventually have changes forced upon it by external events. Overcoming this sort of resistance to change will again require strong leaders that are prepared to change the culture of the organisation and who can lead change from the top. Also needed is a high degree of reassurance built into plans for change as sometimes fears do, in fact, have some foundation. People could be afraid of losing their jobs or of having to learn something new. In this situation extensive communication – and corresponding action – about these matters must be put in place. In addition, fear of the unknown is often an obstacle to innovation and the solution to this is obviously the communication of information. The workforce must be reassured and made to feel more secure. They should be given lots of information about what the proposed changes will involve so that an innovative culture is not smothered by fear. As Sir John Tusa (see the final chapter of this book) comments, 'listening to staff makes the stress much easier to bear as stress can come from being run inefficiently, or being run rigidly.'

Overcoming obstacles to innovation is rarely easy and requires determination, commitment and the ability to communicate the vision, but it is vital that it is done so that the organisation is not left behind. However, although strong leadership is essential, employees must not be ignored. It is highly likely that the workforce will have ideas about what should – and could – change, and possibly have the knowledge about how to go about it, so a good leader will get to know employees and then empower them to overcome obstacles.

Formal proposals

When planning change programmes, a formal business proposal may be deemed necessary for a number of reasons:

- to outline the proposed changes to stakeholders
- to get agreement for funding for a specific change project
- to present to banks or other backers to obtain the necessary finance
- to compete with other departments for resources.

Depending on who it is aimed at, the complexity of the proposals, the size and culture of the organisation and the level of detail that is required, the report should include some or all of the following items.

Summary

A summary of the proposed changes so that readers can quickly get an idea of the report's content and purpose. For some people this may be the only section they need – or want – to read, so it is essential to make this interesting, succinct but comprehensive.

Table of contents

A table of contents is a must if the report runs to more than just a few pages. This will be helpful so that people can focus on what interests them.

Background information

The information that was used to reach the decisions about the changes that are necessary should be included. If there is a lot of information and statistical detail then this can be included in the form of appendices at the end of the report. This information should back up the decisions contained in the report and reinforce the reasons for change and its chances of success.

Details of the changes

A step-by-step explanation of the proposed changes must be given. Include as much detail as necessary here. If the document is to be used for obtaining funding then sufficient detail to convince possible readers that the change has been well thought out and is feasible will be needed. If this is for internal use only then the more detail the better as this may then form the basis of a plan for implementation of the changes at a later date.

The gains to be made

Explain just what would be gained by making the changes. Detail the benefits to be had from the proposed change programme. These can take the form of cost savings, for example, or increased sales and profits and may be both short term and long term.

Time forecasts

A timeline – projected dates for when the proposed changes can be achieved – should be included. This could be either in the form of an explanation of what will happen and when, or it could be a graphical representation of this information.

Resources

The resources required to make the change programme work must be specified. Include explanations of staffing arrangements and how time will be found to carry out the extra work or include an explanation of the external help that will be required, together with a cost breakdown of this. The financial requirements in terms of new equipment, training, technology and so on should also be included. The projected budget for a change programme is often contentious and can be the section that dictates whether or not the programme goes ahead, so close attention should be paid to this aspect of the business proposal. Obviously, in the case of a large change programme with extensive resource requirements, it should be clearly shown that the benefits far outweigh the costs.

Personnel required

A summary of how team members have the right skills and what skills will have to be acquired either through training existing people or bringing in expertise from outside the organisation must be given. If external consultants are to be engaged then the reasoning behind both the need and the choice of consultants will need to be explained.

Good presentation

Make it look professional by presenting the report in an appropriate binder. Make sure that it is checked for errors such as spelling, punctuation and grammar and is read by someone who has not been involved in putting it together so that any areas that are unclear can be amended.

Formulating systems and processes to achieve change

Planning is of key importance at this stage in the change process. The benefits of careful planning are many – there will be less confusion, things will not be forgotten, everyone will know what they have to do, the objectives will be clear, the team will work together better, and progress can be measured and staff motivated – not forgetting a greater chance of success if planning is thorough. There are a number of stages that you should include in your change plan.

Select the team

You will start with a list of the roles that need to be filled. At this stage it is possible that you will already know the majority of employees that will be available to fill them. Matching the two lists – roles and employees – will require some skill and plenty of thought. Assign roles, making sure you have a variety of skills as needed.

Define responsibilities

If you have selected the team carefully and have all the skills in the team (or can arrange timely training), assigning responsibilities will be a straightforward task. It is a good idea to make sure that everyone in the team knows, understands and accepts their responsibilities from the start. This minimises conflict and doubt that may occur if such facts are not made clear early on. This sort of problem can easily delay or derail a change programme if it crops up partway through.

Set goals

It is vital that the goals are adequately communicated to the team. Members should understand exactly what they are expected to achieve and also how they will know when they have achieved it. It is advisable that these goals are discussed face to face with each team member and that they are put down in writing for future reference.

Set milestones

Decide on appropriate points along the road to change – these should cover the key stages of the change plan and will, in effect, give a map of how to get there, including assessments at the appropriate points that will measure progress, ensuring the team is on the right track and on target.

Organise resources

The team leader should ensure that the necessary resources are available. This might include financial resources, sufficient team members to do the work in the time allowed, time allocated during the working day if they are to carry out some of their regular work duties during the change process, and potential extra people and skills that they could call upon if it is found necessary once the plan is underway.

Set up the training that the team needs

Unless your team is highly skilled and all members have carried out this sort of work previously (in which case, why aren't they being stretched by doing something a bit more ambitious?), then some training will be necessary. There should be a budget for this and any training that will help to make the change happen should be organised early on in the process. Don't expect people to just muddle through – give them the right resources.

Review obstacles

A thorough examination of the possible obstacles and problems that the team may face during the change process should be carried out before work begins and the appropriate action that can be taken to deal with them decided upon. The obstacles may vary from resistance to change from members of the team or from people they may come into contact with, to a tight time schedule or a lack of cohesion in the team.

Schedule regular meetings

Having regular meetings to review progress and resolve problems will give everyone in the team the opportunity to air any problems and also help to resolve issues that involve other team members. It will also give the team leader the chance to check on progress. However, it may be necessary for a manager to reinforce attendance at these meetings.

Communicate

This is one of the most important things that will affect the success of any change programme. Make sure that time is planned in to allow you to communicate to your team exactly what you want and for members to let you know how things are going. They will also need to communicate with each other and the systems to allow them to do so must be in place.

Create a work schedule

Here it is necessary to list all the tasks that will need to be carried out in order to achieve the objectives and to monitor progress. The time allowed for each task should be noted in addition to whom the task will be allocated. Care must be taken that the tasks are listed in the right sequence. Dependency relationships between the tasks should also be highlighted so that they are done in the correct order rather than having a delay due to waiting for the results of one task before being able to start another. A Gantt chart can help with scheduling this list of tasks – more about this, including an example of one of these useful charts is given in Chapter 8.

Remember that the opposite of being organised – which is what planning makes you – is chaos. A chaotic approach will not bring about successful change.

There are a number of well-known change systems and ideas that can be used if the proposed change is wide ranging. These are often used if management consultants are brought in to the organisation to bring about the change. Here we consider three of the most common.

Business Process Re-engineering (BPR)

This aims to transform how people work by giving them the processes that will improve business performance. It entails a radical redesign of all the organisation's business processes. Proponents of BPR view an organisation as a series of processes rather than looking at functions such as accounts, sales, marketing and so on.

The first step in BPR is usually to examine and evaluate all current processes before going on to decide the best way to achieve the organisation's aims and objectives. It takes a top-down approach to change by starting with the mission statement so that the purpose and character of the organisation informs the change process. It then considers the vision, i.e. the desired future of the organisation, and builds a business strategy from this point. The process is then continued by setting key performance targets and defining behaviours that will bring about the desired change. In this way BPR can produce key performance measures to track progress and relates efficiency improvements specifically to the culture of the organisation. Specialised software is available to manage the enormous amount of data that a BPR project will inevitably generate.

Total Quality Management (TQM)

This is designed to bring about a gradual process of performance improvement by using a set of principles to arrive at a quality management system that applies throughout the organisation. 'Doing it right first time' is at the centre of TQM philosophy and the principles cover all aspects of quality management including attitudes, behaviour, ethics and culture. TQM must therefore be applied to the whole organisation including aspects that are difficult to measure such as the culture of an organisation or staff attitudes and the ethics applied within the business. TQM can only be used in situations where there is total management commitment to quality improvement in order to achieve increased competitiveness, to reduce waste, create a more productive and satisfying working environment, and to establish a culture of sustainable improvement. It follows eight principles of quality management:

1. Leadership – the purpose and direction must be established by senior management and the environment of the organisation must be lead by the managers. This environment must make it possible for everyone to be committed and fully involved in achieving the objectives of the organisation.

2. Involvement of all employees – it is essential that people at all levels work to the best of their ability to achieve improvements and that an inclusive culture is in place so that the organisation benefits from everyone's abilities.

3. A focus on customers and striving to exceed their expectations – the whole organisation must be focused on customers in this way to ensure customer satisfaction and the ultimate survival of the organisation. Senior managers must be committed to ensuring that every member of staff understands customers' needs.

4. Decisions must be based on analysis of extensive and relevant data – extensive data must be collated and analysed so that change decisions can be factually based.

5. Continual improvement – this must be a permanent objective, with every member of the organisation focused on the need to improve in every area.

6. Mutually beneficial relationships with suppliers – enabling both parties to make improvements and to profit from the relationship.

7. A systems approach – managers should identify all the processes in their organisation or department and understand how they are linked together and interact so that they can manage the whole system. Managing the interrelated processes to achieve an objective ensures that the organisation is effective and efficient.

8. A process approach – managers must treat related resources and activities as a process in order to achieve objectives.

This depth of thinking about quality and change can produce performance improvements because it is necessary to examine all areas of the business in detail, but the level of detail necessary and the data that must be assembled means that it is time consuming and requires a high level of commitment from all concerned. However, an investment of time and other resources in adopting TQM can be repaid by the following:

- a reduction of stress and waste that will result from the new structure
- a greater degree of cooperation between teams
- establishing a new structure according to TQM principles will make growth and survival possible
- the organisation will be made more competitive.

TQM must not be seen as a quick fix as it entails huge changes of culture, organisational processes and management thinking. It can only be successfully implemented where there is management commitment and where a thorough review of the business has been carried out to determine the need for, and direction of, the change. There must be a comprehensive understanding of the business, including consideration of the following:

- the organisation's vision
- its purpose
- its mission
- its values
- its objectives.

When this understanding of the business has been established it must then be communicated to everyone involved in the organisation.

To be successful in establishing the new principles throughout an organisation, TQM must not be viewed as something that can be 'bolted on' to existing management systems, nor must it be seen as a way of getting a certificate that proves it is a 'quality organisation'. Rather it should be viewed as a change in values and culture in an organisation that is fully integrated into the day-to-day activities of the organisation and that will result in improved performance.

Six Sigma

Six Sigma is a business management strategy first developed and used by Motorola in the 1980s to improve its manufacturing processes. It has a set of guidelines aimed at gradual and continuous improvement driven by identifying variations in manufacturing and business processes, and eliminating defects in all areas of an organisation. In Six Sigma terms, a defect is defined as anything that could have a detrimental effect on customer satisfaction. It is a strictly measurement-based and statistical strategy for process improvement and for increasing consistency. The use of Six Sigma does not allow for any assumptions or guesswork.

Not surprisingly, there are six key concepts in Six Sigma:

1. Critical to quality – those attributes that are most important to the organisation's customers.
2. Defect – where the organisation fails to deliver what the customer wants.
3. Process capability – what the organisation's processes are able to deliver.

4. Variation – what the customer sees and feels.
5. Stable operations – ensuring consistent, predictable processes to improve what the customer sees and feels.
6. Design for Six Sigma – designing to meet customer needs and process capability.

Six Sigma is a rigidly controlled methodology under which any project undertaken must make measurable and quantifiable financial returns. It demands strong leadership that is committed not only to improvement but also to supporting the workforce in making those improvements. There are two main ways that it can be put into operation: first on processes that are falling below requirements and need incremental improvement; and second to develop new processes and products.

Using recognised methods of managing quality, such as the three detailed above, can provide a structure for organisational change and will drive improvements due to their emphasis on detailed examination of processes. In recent years the Six Sigma strategy has been combined with lean manufacturing to become Lean Six Sigma and impressive results have been obtained by many large organisations. However, one criticism that has been made of Six Sigma is that it could stifle creativity with its rigid adherence to statistical information.

Practical implementation

Putting a change plan into action should be easier than actually developing the plan. At this point you should just need to follow the plan and if it is sufficiently comprehensive then this will make successful change both easier and far more likely. One area where a manager may meet difficulty is in keeping the team focused on the plan for change when all sorts of other things are happening in the organisation. To assist with the implementation of any plans for change, it is useful to have decided the following in advance of implementation, in addition to the usual objectives and schedules.

Communication methods

Ensure that everyone in the team is kept in the picture and that there are both formal and informal communication systems in place that will facilitate this process. This may include a schedule of major update meetings as well as more frequent briefings. Ensuring that everyone is fully aware of where or who they can go to for information or help during the change project will make things run much more smoothly than merely leaving the team to its own devices.

Define roles and responsibilities

Revised definitions of roles and responsibilities for each member of the team involved in change should be prepared and discussed with individual team members. A formal system of communicating new job descriptions and ensuring that everyone knows who is responsible for the different aspects of the change programme will greatly increase the chances of a successful outcome and will ensure that time is not wasted by uncertainty.

Systems and working methods

The design of new systems and working methods is a crucial part of any change programme and should be in place before commencement.

Training needs

A thorough assessment of the team's training needs (and then prompt provision of the necessary training) will make sure that time is not lost by the inefficient working that results from people not possessing the required skills and knowledge.

Attitudes

A good team leader will know which members of their team have problems with change. As we will discuss in greater detail in Chapter 7, many people will resist change for various reasons and this resistance must be overcome to ensure a smoother change programme with a greater chance of success.

If all these things are in place before the actual work on the change programme starts, it will have a higher chance of success than if they were dealt with as the work goes along. Thorough preparation is essential and will save time and other resources during the life of the programme.

INSTANT TIP

Lead by example. Getting new working methods up and running as soon as possible by the team leader using them is the best way to ensure rapid progress.

As always, communication is the key to ensuring smooth running and all of the aspects of preparation mentioned above should be discussed with the change team. Remember that communication is a two-way process, so that the views and ideas of the team members are taken into account.

Monitoring progress

The monitoring of any change plan should not be viewed as a process that comes at the end of the plan when results are assessed and the success of the completed plan is evaluated, but should be something that goes on at regular intervals to check the work's progress towards the plan's objectives. A system and schedule for monitoring progress should be built into the plan at the initial stages. Monitoring results is an essential part of any innovation project. If you neglect to measure the results, especially in the early stages of a plan, it will be impossible to know if you are on the right track. The methods for measuring the results must be decided when setting the objectives. You must have specific targets set that are quantifiable so that you can be certain whether or not the objectives have been met. It will then be a relatively simple task to compare data from before and after implementation.

However, monitoring progress is not simply about checking figures. It is also about people so it is a good idea to schedule regular meetings where team members have the opportunity to update their manager about progress made and about concerns they may have about how things are going. It is also an opportunity to celebrate results achieved so far. This is all part of the process of keeping a team motivated and on track.

Of course, if you find that your objectives are not being met, you will need to have contingency plans in place to put things right. These can be the result of a brainstorming session with your team where you look at everything that could go wrong and develop a solution to the problem to be used if it should occur. Above all, do not be tempted simply to measure your results over time and then ignore the data produced. Monitoring is only useful if action is taken in response to the results.

SUMMARY

This chapter dealt with some of the practical aspects of introducing change and innovation. We reviewed the resources needed – capital, time, expertise, technology and, above all, commitment and enthusiasm.

Next we looked at removing obstacles to innovation including inertia, a lack of leadership, sticking to tradition and fear of change.

A formal proposal is sometimes necessary, especially for larger change programmes and we examined what should be included.

Next we dealt with the stages of planning a change programme including selecting a team, defining its roles, setting goals and objectives, reviewing and putting in place training and the necessary resources. It is also advisable to identify and deal with possible obstacles in advance and to schedule meetings so that communication is planned into the work schedule which should be prepared at this stage.

This was followed by brief details of three change systems that are often used if management consultants are engaged to oversee major changes – i.e. Business Process Re-engineering (BPR), Total Quality Management (TQM) and Six Sigma.

Finally, we noted the importance of thorough preparation to smooth the progress of the change programme and of monitoring progress to ensure objectives are met.

ACTION CHECKLIST

1. Consider the relative importance of the resources needed for change – capital, time, expertise, technology and commitment. Are they all of equal importance?
2. Why are many people afraid of change?
3. What do you think should be the priorities when selecting a team for a change programme?
4. Why is it better to put training in place at the start of a change programme?
5. What do you think would happen if communication was neglected in the planning of a change programme?

06

How can you manage change?

Managing change, as we have said previously, is part of any manager's role. Learning how to accept change and then manage it efficiently will undoubtedly improve a manager's performance in any organisation. Change will come whether or not we look for it and plan it, so being able to manage it is vital.

Communicating reasons for change

The single most important action a manager can take is to ensure that all members of the team fully understand, and are behind, any change programme that is implemented. If the team understands the thinking that is driving the change then they are far more likely to accept it and get on with its implementation. Resistance, as we will discuss in the next chapter, is born of fear and fear can be dispelled with knowledge and understanding. There are four main points that must be communicated to staff in the event of any change process:

1. Why? What will happen if we stay as we are?
2. The reasons behind the change. The drivers of the change need to be made clear. This may be a changing market that has caused a product change, falling profits, or a customer survey that highlighted problems in customer service for example.
3. What? Details of the change and how it will affect employees and their work roles must be communicated. Done properly, communicating this aspect of a change programme may help to allay the fears that some staff may have.
4. When? The reasons why the change must happen now must be communicated so that people do not think that the change is not urgent and that work on it could be delayed if necessary. People will always procrastinate if there is something to be done that is not entirely to their taste so the manager must make sure that all his team members understand the urgency and what will happen if the change is not made without delay.

Obviously, when communicating the need for change it is necessary for a manager to put a positive spin on it and to explain the advantages of the change and the disadvantages of not changing. This will need a confident delivery from the manager and an upbeat attitude to the changes, added to real commitment and enthusiasm.

A vision of the future can be created at this point. A manager should outline the objectives of the change and show team members, as comprehensively and convincingly as possible, the gains that could be made that will provide advantages for both the team and the organisation.

Having painted this picture of a positive future, the manager should then go on to explain exactly how the team can help. Members need to understand and accept the part they have to play in the success of the change programme and the work that they will have to take on.

After all this information has been communicated, team members should be given the opportunity to ask questions and to digest what they have been told. The manager will then need to check the team's understanding and commitment to what is planned and deal with any problems that may arise – whether these are from lack of understanding or lack of motivation.

Done well, communicating the reasons for change to a team embarking upon a change programme can make the chances of success much greater.

Setting objectives

It is essential to most people to understand what is expected of them in their work role. Similarly, any organisation needs to be clear where it is going if it is to be successful. In both these cases setting objectives provides the way forward. Objectives will help an organisation to:

- improve performance
- show staff where to focus their efforts
- illustrate the vision for the organisation
- provide direction
- motivate staff
- measure performance
- highlight priorities.

As always, for any objectives that are set in organisations, objectives related to innovation must be SMART – Specific, Measurable, Achievable, Realistic and Timely. In addition, if objectives are to encourage innovation and help to facilitate change they must look forward to the results of current work rather than relying on work that has been done previously. So, for example, when setting objectives based on sales of a product, it must be possible to measure the extra sales that have resulted from current innovative efforts rather than confusing them with sales that have resulted from previous marketing.

The objectives that are set during an innovation process must be directly related to the results required from the innovation. This process is the move from where an organisation is today to where it wants to be at a specified future time. It will be useful at this stage to look at examples of objectives that can be set to specifically encourage innovation. Here are examples of such objectives that could be set to lead innovation:

- launch three new products in the next financial year
- find two new suppliers of the main production component
- gain entry to two new overseas markets
- implement an employee suggestion scheme and achieve at least two suggestions from each team member within three months.

As you can see, the idea is to encourage something new – new ideas, new customers, new markets, new suppliers and new ways of doing things – and objectives can be closely tailored to the vision of the organisation. The number of objectives set must be carefully controlled – too many will be unwieldy and confusing, too few will mean that innovation is not encouraged in all areas.

Dealing with expectations

Everyone connected with an organisation will have their own expectations – from customers and suppliers to stakeholders and staff. Let's look at what some of these expectations may be.

Customers will expect ...

... improved product ranges and better quality at lower prices in the quantities that they require, when they require them.

Shareholders will demand ...

... a better return on their investment, improved share values and increased dividend payments. If they don't get these it is likely that they will take their investments wherever more commitment to improvement is evident.

Staff will be looking for ...

... better pay and working environment, plus extra rewards and incentives as well as improved career paths. They will also be looking for loyalty and commitment from their employers.

In short, everyone will expect improvements. But not all these expectations will be met. If an organisation attempts to meet any, or all, of these expectations with short-term solutions this will usually only result in short-term satisfaction. For example, products can be re-branded or tweaked to offer customers something that appears different and improved but in the long term customers will reject the 'new' products and will take their custom to an organisation that has something genuinely innovative to offer.

However, there is still the problem of keeping everyone motivated while going through a change programme. Staff can quickly become de-motivated and start to slow down or even work against the changes if they believe that they are not going to be successful, and shareholders and backers will become wary if changes do not happen as quickly as they had hoped and produce the benefits they had expected.

It is important here to be clear what expectations are. They are not just your customer's or your team member's requirements. They are not even the objectives of any change project. And usually they are not stated, but are held in the mind of the person with the expectation. They are a vision of the future built up in a number of ways.

Although it is usually important to manage expectations there is an alternative view that holds that modest expectations lead to modest results. If demanding targets are set, then this will bring about a different type of thinking compared with totally achievable targets. For example, given a modest target a marketing manager may simply tweak a product range, relaunch it and achieve the limited sales growth asked of her, whereas if she had been given a challenging target she may have had to think of something far more radical in order to achieve it and may have come up with a genuinely innovative product range. It is therefore probable that setting high expectations, but managing the situation well and keeping the workforce motivated will create an environment where people can think creatively and where innovation will flourish.

Managing risk

If you are a manager or team leader, or hoping to be one in the future, then there is one thing of which you can be sure of – things will go wrong on a regular basis. Managing risk is therefore an important aspect of managing change. Risk is taken on in business when not everything is known about a situation – the less that is known, the higher the risk. Whatever is known about a situation, or can be found out, gives information that can be used to eliminate or minimise risk. So, risk management involves identifying what could go wrong and putting in place strategies to deal with those risks with the aim of minimising the effect on the business. It is far more cost effective to plan how to deal with something in advance of it happening than to do nothing and be unprepared. When an organisation is about to implement a change programme risk management becomes more important, so we will look at how this can be done.

As with all management processes, risk management is a series of actions that can be planned.

Identification

The organisation must first identify the risks that could affect the business. These risks may be financial, operational or market based. We will look in a bit more detail at the types of risk that can be managed later in this section.

Evaluation

Having identified the risks, an organisation must then assess the likelihood of the risk actually occurring and decide whether to accept the risk or plan action to minimise or eradicate it. The considerations here are:

1. What is the consequence of this risk?
2. What is the probability of this risk?

Having answered these two questions, managers can then go on to decide how the risk will be dealt with and whether the cost of eliminating or minimising the risk outweighs the cost of it being allowed to happen.

Developing systems

Having understood the risks, the organisation must then formulate plans to deal with the problems that would be caused.

Monitoring

As always, any systems must be monitored to check their effectiveness. This will ensure that the risks identified are still current and relevant, show that the plans to deal with specific risks work and that the risks are being effectively dealt with.

The types of risk that can be managed can be, as we said earlier, broken down into three broad groups:

1. Financial – this includes things such as the risk of a large customer going out of business while he owes money to the company or fraud by an employee. Of course, all organisations are subject to the risks of the general financial markets – after all, as the saying goes, investments can go down as well as up.

2. Operational – this includes types of risk that will affect an organisation's ability to produce the goods and services that are at the centre of its business. Examples of this type of risk include theft of equipment from the organisation or the breakdown of a vital piece of machinery, labour problems and so on.

3. Market-based – these are risks of things that happen in the market that the company operates in. An example of this type of risk would be if market demand changes substantially or if a new competitor comes into the market.

Case study

A small, independent supplier of office equipment to small businesses throughout the country decided to implement a risk management policy. They proceeded to list all the things that could possibly go wrong in the business and then set about creating a contingency plan and putting in place safeguards in each area.

During the assessment the supplier realised that its information technology was a particularly vulnerable area. After extensive research it put in place a number of regular back-ups for the systems that were in operation. There would have been serious problems for the business if the systems had malfunctioned for any reason and data were lost.

As part of its risk management strategy the supplier also assessed the insurance situation in each area and decided that it would be cost effective to cover its senior sales manager with a 'key man' policy so that the financial costs involved of losing this person could be recouped.

When the risk management strategy had been in place for a number of months, the managing director of the business reviewed it and stated that it had been a success in that it had taken some of the worry out of situations and had avoided the 'fire-fighting' approach that many of his fellow business managers took. The supplier has now scheduled twice yearly reviews of the risks faced by the business and how it would deal with problems if they arose.

Apart from implementing a risk management programme, an organisation can also insure against many of the risks that may affect its business and this will serve to lessen the financial impact. Risks that can be insured against by a business include:

- Fire – a serious fire in office or factory buildings can put a business out of operation for a long period, so this is essential. This would be part of a policy that covered the buildings.
- Theft – the cost of replacing large items of machinery, tools, stock and goods in transit could be prohibitive so this insurance cover is also vital.
- Public liability – this offers cover for events such as someone being injured while on your premises or any third party claim made against the organisation.
- Employer's liability – this is a legal requirement even if the organisation employs only one person. It covers the organisation for legal costs and for claims made by employees who are injured at work or who may have been made ill by their employment.
- Motor vehicles – again, this is compulsory if an organisation operates vehicles on the road and it will cover against damage to the vehicle itself or people hurt in an accident and against legal costs that may arise from use of the vehicle (not including, of course, speeding or parking fines).
- Interruption to business – this can usually be covered by a specially designed policy. It will cover, for example, losses incurred when machinery is damaged.
- Products liability – this covers an organisation against claims relating to the use of its products.
- Key personnel – if there are a limited number of people on whom the whole organisation's successful running depends, then losing them can be insured against.

Although the cost of some insurance policies can be very high, the cost of putting things right if the worst does happen can put an organisation out of business so insurance should be part of any risk management process.

Benefits of risk management

Risk management brings many benefits to an organisation by:

- improving the chances of a change programme succeeding
- reducing the amount of time spent on emergency action
- assisting in the efficient allocation of resources
- improving planning and decision making
- preventing serious loss.

However, not all risks can be predicted and managed so all organisations will, at some time, have to deal with unexpected problems. The next section deals with this aspect of change management.

Dealing with the unexpected

In any management situation the unexpected will happen. Change programmes can be derailed by a variety of events and it is a manager's job to deal with the disruption or problem and to ensure that the project remains on track. The unexpected situations could be put into five categories:

1. Mistakes in the original information

If the plans for change have been built on information that is incorrect there will be problems when the mistake is discovered. For example, if a new customer service system has been planned based on an estimated number of incoming calls, then the plans will have to be revised – changes made to the number of call handlers or to the call handling system may be needed – if in reality there are many more or a lot fewer calls than had been estimated. This sort of unexpected situation requires immediate changes to the planned programme so that improvements can still be achieved.

2. Underestimations of how long things will take

Scheduling the tasks to be carried out in a change programme is something that must be done very carefully, with a realistic view of how long things will take. If there are serious underestimations then work will quickly fall behind and the programme will be in danger of not meeting its objectives.

3. Changes imposed by senior management

This is often the most difficult situation to deal with as it can cause confusion and be demoralising to those working on the changes. If employees feel that they have been asked to do one thing and then find that the direction of the project has been changed, they may feel that management is incompetent. Obviously, this will need careful handling. If senior managers have imposed a change that affects the work being done then it should be their responsibility to explain exactly why they have taken the action. However, it will sometimes happen that a team manager running a change programme will simply be told of a change to policy or finances, for example, and then expected to get on with it. In this case, the manager must make sure that as much detail as possible of the imposed changes to the programme is communicated to the team.

The team manager will need to explain the effect of the decision and, if possible, why it had to be made. It will then be necessary to revise the plans, taking into account the senior management's changes and make sure the team know exactly what its new duties, responsibilities and objectives are. It is important also at this stage to rebuild the team's confidence.

4. Problems in the team

The behaviour of just one team member can disrupt an entire change programme; or it may be that allegiances have been formed within the team that are cutting out some members and hampering progress. If the problem is limited to one disruptive team member then the team's manager will need to counsel that member and find out the reasons behind the problem behaviour. The manager's expectations must be made clear and a suitable solution arrived at, including an agreed action plan for the team member to follow. Unless the solution is complete removal of the problem member from the team, it will be necessary to follow up the discussion with that team member and to check periodically that the solution has proved successful. If the problem is that 'mini-teams' have been formed within the main team then the manager will need to make a judgement as to how disruptive this is. Some allegiances can be beneficial but many can cause problems if members of an allegiance, in effect, make their own rules.

It is a manager's job to ensure that all team or department members are working towards the joint goal that has been agreed. If it is found that some people are 'off message' then they will need to be brought into line before the whole team is badly affected. At this point it can be useful to increase the frequency of team meetings to restate the objectives and ensure that the change can go ahead as planned. It may also be useful to run team building exercises such as brainstorming sessions to deal with the problems that have been encountered, or plan social events that will enhance the cohesiveness of the team.

5. Problems from other teams

Problems from within your own organisation but not from within your team could centre on a lack of cooperation with what is required to make your change programme a success. This may be a request for information that is not acted upon and may require the manager of a department handling a change programme to step in to avoid unnecessary delays. Sometimes the intervention of authority is enough, while at other times a new system for getting access to information may need to be set up or a conversation may need to be had further up the chain of command. After intervention of this sort, it is important that the manager monitors future communications between the two departments to ensure that the problem has been resolved completely.

Case study

An unusual mistake occurred when an airline decided to try to stop pilfering of spirits miniatures. It suspected that its onboard staff were taking the drinks for their own use so the airline set a trap to prove this. They rigged an alarm clock to the door of the locker where the bottles were kept with the idea that the clock would stop when the door was opened, thus proving the time when the theft took place. However, a member of staff heard the alarm clock ticking, thought there was a bomb on board and alerted other staff. The captain took the decision to make an emergency landing.

This cost the airline many thousands of pounds and the lesson that should be learned is to thoroughly assess all possible outcomes of any plans before putting them into operation.

Uncovering problems

Whatever unexpected situation crops up when trying to deal with change, it will need to be dealt with. The manager of the team or department will need to revise plans where necessary and do everything possible to keep the team on track. It is essential that problems are not ignored and, even if the manager has dealt with the issue, communication about it with the team is vital. Regular evaluation should always be part of any change programme (more about this in Chapter 8) and this should continue throughout the changes. This may be how the unexpected is discovered.

There are several questions that can be asked to ensure that any problems are uncovered:

- Are we on target with the plans?
- If not, why not?
- Where are we having problems?
- What, if anything, is hindering progress?
- Is everything happening as we expected and planned?

Where changes to the original plans have become necessary because of unexpected events, the manager and team will need to revise the plans to take account of the changes caused. This may include changes to resources such as the number of team members required to effect the change, the timescales, financial implications and any extra training that may be needed. In the case of the most severe changes to plans this may almost be like going back to the beginning and starting again. But, of course, it is a manager's job to deal with these problems as they arise.

It is clear that dealing with problems earlier is preferable to ignoring them (or being unaware of them) thereby letting the effects build up and the problems becoming embedded. The key to success in this area is to have systems set up so that managers get early warning of things going wrong. These should cover all important areas of the organisation including:

- Markets – data should be obtained on a regular basis regarding both customer and competitor activity. Data should be supplied internally in the form of sales reports, surveys and so on and also externally by way of media reports and updates from Chambers of Commerce and trade associations.
- Technology – all managers need to be aware of developments in technology that could change how they do things or that their competitors may use to gain an advantage.
- Costs – keeping control of costs is essential to any organisation's success and is easier if regular updates are available.
- Cashflow – careful examination of cash received and cash outstanding will enable managers to prevent this becoming a problem. Poor cashflow is a common cause of small or new businesses failing so keeping this under control is particularly important.
- Staff – details should be regularly examined regarding rates of absenteeism, staff retention and the number of disputes and grievances. On a less quantifiable level, managers need to be aware of discontent among staff and the reason for possible grievances.
- Suppliers – early warnings of delays in deliveries should be demanded from important suppliers and a check kept on price levels.
- Production – data supplied by production departments regarding machine output and output per man hour should be examined in detail on a regular basis to ensure that production problems can be resolved before they affect profitability.

The key to these early warning systems is obtaining the right data on a regular basis and, above all, understanding and using it. Spotting trends is a key management skill that can head off many potential problems.

Learning from mistakes

The best way to deal with mistakes is, of course, not to make them in the first place. Most problems can be foreseen so it is important not to skimp on the amount of time or other resources that are put into the planning of a change programme. Plenty of time spent before the start of a project can identify possible pitfalls and save time later down the line. Consider the following during the planning stage.

What could go wrong?

What is the worst that could go wrong? It may be that the programme's budget is particularly rigid and to go over that budget would be a major disaster so the answer is to double check all expenditure and make it clear to team members that any extra expenditure must be authorised by the team leader or senior manager. Alternatively, it may be that of several goals of the change programme, one is viewed as more important than the others – so give that goal extra attention and perhaps review progress towards it more frequently.

Are the goals achievable?

Are they too ambitious? Does achieving them require 100 per cent perfection? Although it is always best to aim for the best, it must be accepted that things will go wrong – a key team member could leave or be taken ill or changes outside the organisation may take place that have an effect on the change programme, for example. There must therefore be some leeway in the plans. If goals are completely unachievable, team members could easily be de-motivated and incorporating over-optimistic goals will not help anybody.

Check priorities

Decide what is important. If achieving the change in the shortest possible time is the most important constraint on the programme then urgency must be given extra attention. There will be other priorities such as cost or performance that constrain the programme and it is useful to decide the things that are not as important and then to establish a degree of flexibility in the less important areas.

If problems can be taken into account at the initial stages of the programme, then it is far more likely that goals will be achieved. However, there will rarely be a change programme that runs smoothly from start to finish and during which no mistakes at all are made so it is important to learn from them and to put them right as soon as they are spotted. They will not usually put themselves right and will often get worse if left. So, how can you put mistakes right and ensure that they are not repeated?

Mistakes during change programmes can fall into five broad categories:

1. Budgetary – not having allowed sufficient resources for all that it is planned to achieve can cause problems during the life of the programme. For example, if there is a lack of funds to buy the technology or machinery that is deemed necessary in order to effect the changes successfully, then there will be a dilemma to resolve: should the projected results be scaled back, the budget increased or savings made in other areas of the project? The team leader will need to understand fully the priorities of the stakeholders of the change programme. It may be that finishing on time is the most important thing to achieve or the budget could be extremely restricted with no chance of increasing the amount spent on the

changes. Only when these priorities have been assessed can a decision about what action to take be made.

2. Insufficient research or knowledge – during a change programme the unexpected will always happen and a competent team leader will always consider whether or not they should have been able to foresee the problem. In many situations where mistakes are made they could have been avoided if the team had had sufficient knowledge before the project started. Once the mistake has been made, however, it is vital that this problem is addressed. This may entail extra training or more market research.

3. Rigid plans – it is absolutely vital during any improvement programme to be flexible. Good planning is important, of course, but there should always be 'room to manoeuvre'. Market conditions or internal priorities may change during the life of the change programme so any team leader or senior manager must be prepared to revise the plans to take into account the current situation. It is a mistake to stick rigidly to the original plans if they are no longer the best way forward. Continual adjustment will be necessary.

4. Attitudes – having members of the team who are against the change can quickly derail a programme. If a mistake occurs as a result of a poor attitude from a member of the team then that person will need to either leave the team or be brought fully into it. The decision for the team leader to make here is whether or not that team member can be replaced reasonably easily or whether it is feasible to change the attitude through communication and/or training.

5. Human error – these occur in all types of work. It is almost impossible to avoid them completely but close supervision where necessary and regular meetings to discuss progress will ensure that these errors are not allowed to seriously affect the outcome of the change programme.

Obviously, many of the errors that occur during a change programme could be avoided but the solutions when problems occur after the planning stage are usually fairly straightforward. Decisions will, however, have to be made without delay when problems are encountered. For example, if changes in the market occur then the team leader will have to assess how this will affect the planned changes and be prepared to make a change of direction if necessary or if underestimations are made regarding the amount of time required for parts of the programme, then either more staff will have to be brought on board or time saved in other areas to keep to the deadlines set. This type of assessment, decision making and re-planning is a fundamental part of a team leader's role when managing a change programme and learning from mistakes is essential if successful projects are to be managed in the future.

Giving useful feedback

Part of a manger's role is to give feedback to team members in order to enhance performance, reinforce productive behaviour and eliminate behaviour that is hampering the team or the individual's performance. This feedback should be frequent, relevant, constructive and timely. Team members should always appreciate the usefulness of the feedback although the parts of it that refer to negative behaviour or results will not usually be easy to take, and the best way of ensuring constructive and well-received feedback is to incorporate regular feedback sessions into your management style.

There are a few aspects of giving feedback that it is useful to remember:

● Give individual feedback face to face and one to one. Very few people feel comfortable receiving feedback in public and even if it is positive feedback the effect may be counterproductive. If you try to give feedback by telephone then you will not be able to judge the person's reactions as well as you would if you were face to face.

- Team feedback should be delivered to the team. If it is negative feedback then this will give the team the chance to come up with a solution to a problem or a way of improving its performance and if it is positive feedback then the team's achievement should be recognised collectively.
- Make it specific. Generalisations are never as effective as specific examples.
- Feedback must be sincere. Don't try to hoodwink your team with a bit of flattery. This will not have the motivating effect that you were perhaps hoping for.
- Make it comprehensive. If you have arranged a feedback session with a member of your team then you will need to cover all aspects of their work – how they have performed, how they have behaved, how they related to other team members and so on.
- Give both positive and negative feedback – not just one or the other.
- Make it regular and frequent. Team members should feel that they always know how they are doing. Also, they need to be able to make changes as necessary after each feedback session so that problems are not allowed to go unchecked.

Giving useful feedback is an important part of a manager's role that can be beneficial to both the team and to the individual if given correctly. It can provide many opportunities for a proactive manager to act as a team coach.

SUMMARY

In this chapter we discussed how to manage change and started with the most important aspect – communication. It is essential to let everyone involved know why the change is needed, what will happen and when. *(Continued)*

(Continued)

We then looked at setting objectives for innovation to encourage something new such as generating new ideas, gaining new customers or breaking into new markets.

Dealing with everyone's expectations is an essential element of managing change as is managing risk, which involves identifying and evaluating risks then developing plans to deal with possible problems. Monitoring these plans is, as always, necessary. The three types of risk were classified as financial, operational and market-based.

While contingency plans should always be in place, the unexpected can happen. The causes include mistakes made in the original information, underestimating the length of time needed, changes imposed, team difficulties and problems within the organisation.

Next, we looked at the effect of mistakes and problems that occur during a change process and how to avoid or resolve them. Finally, we dealt with how to give useful feedback by making it comprehensive, regular, sincere and specific, and delivering it one to one.

ACTION CHECKLIST

1. Why is communication the most important element in the change process?
2. What sort of objectives could you set to help your organisation break in to new markets?
3. Name three types of risk that you know your organisation is insured against.
4. Consider the members of a team of which you have been – or are – a member. Do any of them cause problems? What is their attitude to change?
5. Think about the last time you received feedback from your manager – was it positive or negative and how did it make you feel?

07

Why do people oppose change?

Change is, almost without exception, difficult and the main reason is people's opposition to change. People often feel threatened by possible changes. They will worry about the consequences and may go to some lengths to avoid it – or even to sabotage it. Obviously, for anyone trying to lead or implement change this is an obstacle that must be overcome. Unless all the people involved in organisational change can be made to understand and support the change, then there will be a much reduced chance of success. In this chapter we will look at some of the reasons for this fear and opposition, examining some of the ways in which this can be dealt with.

At this point it is useful to note that this fear is not confined to people to whom change happens – it is often also felt by the people who have to decide upon, plan and implement change in organisations. As we said in earlier chapters, change is inevitable so all managers will have to deal with it and, if they have some of the natural feelings that make them feel antipathy towards change, then this must be overcome.

The psychology of change

Change can result in a variety of psychological effects including the two main ones – arousal and loss of control. In the initial stages people will be aroused by change. This has both positive and negative behavioural effects. The positive effects include curiosity and excitement at what may be about to happen. This will carry some of the workforce along in the early stages of change but may not last long enough to bring about any real change benefits. The negative effects include fear plus confusion and tension. As the change process continues, fatigue may set in and performances will decline. This deterioration in performance will affect morale, problem-solving skills, communication and negativity, and this in turn leads to a loss of control of the project. With loss of control comes a range of emotions, all of which can lead to an attempt to sabotage (whether consciously or sub-consciously) the change process and these emotions include aggression, stress and anxiety. Any manager planning a change project in an organisation must be aware of these emotions and allow time and resources in the plans for the necessary communication, extra time to do the work and training that will help people to deal with both their emotions and the change. This will avoid some of the problems that will result from people's psychological reactions to change.

Of course, all managers will also have to deal with their own feelings about change, and an awareness of how change commonly affects people will help with this. It is a manager's job, during a change project, to ensure they maintain a positive attitude both individually and in the workforce. It is essential that managers do all they can to create a working environment where everyone is able to make sense of what is going on and to cope with the changes. If change is simply imposed, without sufficient discussion, consultation and explanation, then most people will have far more difficulty in reacting positively.

As a counterpoint to this rather pessimistic-sounding aspect of change, it can be useful to note that some people – especially if the change process is well-managed – will actually welcome change. The reasons for this may include:

- Taking on a new challenge – many people look for a challenge in their working lives.
- It is good experience. Going through a major change programme in an organisation can be viewed as something that will enhance career prospects and give valuable experience that can, if necessary, be put to good use in other organisations.
- If the team leader is respected and has the confidence of the team, then team members may willingly follow the leader through any change programme.
- Change may make work more interesting.
- If team members have been closely involved with the decision to make a change and in planning that change, they will feel that they own it and will willingly play their part.
- If people are fully convinced that the change will produce appreciable benefits for themselves as well as for the organisation, then they will welcome it.

It is obvious from this last section that although many people fear change, there are others that will welcome it. In any event the change must be well managed if it is to be successful. Overcoming the various barriers to change is a starting point for managing change and that is what we will cover in the next section.

Overcoming barriers

First let's look at what the barriers to change are. Many of these barriers are put up by people who simply do not want to change and this is the focus of this chapter. However, there are lots of external and internal obstacles and we will examine them briefly here. These can be termed **operational barriers** and include the following.

A stable organisation

When things have remained the same for many years this can become a barrier to change. Tradition can be a strong force against change and where things have been done in the same way for years, in an environment that encourages an old-fashioned outlook and a pride in keeping up traditional values, change can be more difficult to achieve. Extra work will have to be done to explain the need for change and to convince people that the organisation will be improved by the change. As always, it will be necessary to explain what will happen if the organisation does not change.

Relocation

Where a change of premises becomes necessary in order to take the business forward, the problems that come with relocation will sometimes become a barrier to change. These problems will include the possible loss of key members of the workforce who may not be willing, or able, to travel to the new premises, transferring and reinstalling machinery, the training that may become necessary for new staff in the new location, extra costs incurred and so on.

Technology

Old technology can keep an organisation mired in an ever-worsening situation where meaningful change without appreciable investment in new technology becomes impossible. There may be a reluctance to spend on new technology and also on the extensive training that will become necessary.

Systems

This could also be referred to as bureaucracy. Where an organisation is large and is structured and controlled in a bureaucratic manner then change will be difficult to achieve. Extensive training in new systems will be necessary and widespread communication efforts will have to be made to overcome the inertia that a bureaucratic system can produce.

Success

If an organisation is perceived as successful and has functioned well over a long period of time, then creating the impetus for change will be hard. This is the 'if it isn't broke, don't fix it' syndrome and a case will have to be made for the improvements that can be made over the long term.

Failure

Conversely, failure as well as success can be a barrier to change. If changes have been tried and have failed in the past then it can be difficult to try again. Managers may back off any drastic changes when they have seen the response that change has produced previously and it may be difficult to motivate them to lead the changes. Other members of the workforce who have seen the results of previous change initiatives will also be sceptical.

Fear of unemployment

Although this fear is part of the behavioural group of barriers to be discussed next, it is also an operational fear in that senior managers will often want to avoid the situation where they will have to make people redundant and this may stand in the way of change plans.

All of these operational barriers will cause change to be delayed or avoided altogether and it is management's job to overcome these barriers. At the same time, they will have to take into account a second set of barriers – ones related to **behaviour** and **people's feelings**. These can include the following.

Lack of understanding

If the workforce does not have sufficient detail about what is happening and what the objectives of the change are, then they will not support it. They will not have confidence in the change and this will result in a resistance to change and poor performance.

Fear

When change is planned, there will always be fear among the workforce. There does not always have to be a concrete reason for the fear but people will often fear a loss of status or will simply experience a fear of the unknown. The antidote to this, of course, is communication. When they know and understand what will happen and how it will affect them, most people will lose some of the fear they feel.

Insecurity

This is, of course, linked to fear but is a fear of something specific. People undergoing change or who know that change is imminent, will often worry that their jobs will disappear or will be made so difficult that they will not be able to carry out their work roles with any success. Again, an explanation of the predicted outcomes of the change will help.

Familiarity

There is a natural impulse to stay with what you know and when changes are proposed the current situation can quickly be reasoned into becoming something that is perfect and therefore does not need changing.

'Office politics'

In many organisations there will be internal barriers caused by how different departments and teams deal with each other. Sometimes people become very protective of themselves and their work group and they will guard information, keeping it to themselves instead of sharing it. This is because they may fear that letting others in on a discovery they have made or a way of doing something will give the advantage to another team or individual. This is a self-defensive action. There will inevitably be rivalry and competition between departments but this cannot be allowed to impede innovation and change.

All of these behavioural factors will result in a resistance to change that needs to be overcome if change and improvement are to be achieved.

Communicating with your team

The most important tool that a manager has in overcoming either operational or behavioural barriers is communication and the thing to remember about communication is that it must be two-way – managers should listen to what staff are saying and not just tell them what they want them to hear. Let's look briefly at the main principles of effective communication.

Communication must be easy to understand

This is the first rule of communication. It is important to remember who the communication is aimed at. Using language that can be understood by the target audience is essential. The message must be clear – if there is any suggestion that there is a hidden message or that the full information has not been given, then this will result in suspicion and a diluting of the effectiveness of the message. Rather than digesting and acting upon the real message, people will start to wonder – and to discuss between themselves – exactly what the communication really meant and what is being hidden from them. This can be avoided by adopting a straightforward tone in memos, emails, meetings and discussions.

Keep it positive

Communication must be positive whenever possible – if the tone of the communication is positive then there is a far greater chance that the recipients will take action. If the communication is negative, then people may simply ignore it at best, or will be discouraged by it at worst. However, if negative news does have to be conveyed, then it should be kept short, clear and precise.

Make it direct

All communications must be direct – this again is in an attempt to ensure that communications are not viewed with suspicion and produce a negative reaction. The impression that something is being hidden must be avoided and a direct, straightforward approach is the best way to do this. Keep to the point.

Keep it brief

Communications must be as brief as possible – in recent years they have become shorter. News reports are, in some cases, limited to little more than headlines while letters, memos, emails and many books are dominated by brief bullet points in an effort to convey information as quickly as possible. And consider the discipline of messages on Twitter, the social networking website, where messages, or 'tweets' are limited to just 140 characters. With online communications it is generally accepted that people cannot be bothered to read large chunks of text. This all means that communications in our working lives must be concise. Long, rambling memos, emails and meetings will not get the message across as effectively as a concise, to-the-point item.

Written communications, must be succinct and unambiguous as there will often be no opportunity to query what has been asserted. Also, all the reader has to go on is what is on the paper – they cannot judge what you mean by your tone of voice or appearance. Good written communication will follow these rules:

- Keep to the point.
- Say exactly what you mean.
- Don't use jargon.
- Use some 'white space' so that the layout does not look cluttered.
- Avoid sarcasm – it does not come over well in written communication.
- When you've finished writing the message, check it – does it say what you mean, are the spelling, punctuation and grammar OK?

As we said, communication must be two-way. A manager must receive information from the team as well as transmit it; and must be receptive to the messages that a team will be giving out. Listening skills are an important part of any manager's skills set.

Listening in the following way will help:

- Pay full attention – don't try to think up counter arguments as this will disrupt your concentration.
- Make eye contact – but don't glare or intimidate.
- Don't interrupt without good reason.
- Note the main points that are being made and try to relate them to what you already know.
- Think rationally, not emotionally.
- Make allowances for people who are perhaps not as articulate as you are – they still have a point to make.
- When the person has finished speaking, summarise what they have said. This will help you to understand and will also show the speaker that you have understood them.

Of course, messages can be conveyed in more ways than simply verbally. Body language and actions taken must also be noted. If, for example, someone looks restless when you are speaking, consider whether it means they are bored, need a break, they've lost track of what you were saying or are impatient to put their own message across. And if members of your team agree with everything you say but then do the opposite of what you wanted them to, you will have to review your own communication skills.

Office politics

Dealing with office politics is often difficult, as the natural competition between departments can be something that assists the organisation if it leads teams to strive for improvements. However, in many cases it can be very damaging and where it may stand in the way of change, it must be dealt with. There are a number of ways that this can be done.

Encourage competition

As competition is the positive side of office politics it can be beneficial to capitalise on this by setting up innovation challenges. Here, different departments can compete to find the biggest savings resulting from innovation or to see which department can come up with the most ideas for change.

Encourage social activities

Anything that gets people together – either within their teams or cross-departmentally – will help them to bond and will increase the amount of idea sharing. Encouraging people to take their lunch together or laying on an 'away day' for staff where they can take part in an activity together will help to forge alliances that can ensure that barriers to change are broken down.

Keep people informed

Make plenty of information about the different teams' activities and successes available (perhaps via newsletters or the organisation's intranet) – the more everyone knows about what is going on in different departments, the less can be hidden.

Plan activities

Activities such as brainstorming sessions, change programmes and special projects that are specifically made up with members from different teams can all help to break down barriers and foster understanding – rather than enmity – between different teams and departments.

When the type of unhealthy competition and negative communication that comes with office politics is allowed to become entrenched, then the effects on communication within the organisation will be severely detrimental. If, in the efforts that go in to protecting their individual positions or departments, members of staff begin to guard information and treat it as a resource to be traded or restricted to the 'chosen few', then it is the manager's responsibility to disseminate information as widely and by as many methods as possible to break this hold. People can begin to treat information as a source of influence and management will have lost control if this is allowed to happen.

Transforming behaviour

There are two aspects to transforming behaviour. One is that despite the fact that there may be many team members who feel uneasy and insecure about change, you will still need to get all your staff working in a positive direction towards change. The other is that you may have one or more members of the team who are actively working against the proposed changes. Let's look first at ways in which you can motivate your team so that they are not daunted by change.

There are three main ways in which, if you are the manager who has to make change happen, you can get your team to view the change more positively and so avoid some of the problems that can be caused by negative attitudes to change. First, as we have said so many times, you must communicate. The more your team know, the less likely members are to be afraid, uncooperative or behave negatively. Also, if the team feels involved and you can show that you value its input then there will be a far greater chance of success. Second, you will need to gain your team's full cooperation. You will, of course, have to have built up its trust in you as a leader prior to the change programme but how you deal with members during the planning stage and the duration of a change programme will also affect how they feel about the change. Third, you must try to develop a cohesive team. In this way the optimistic, reliable members of your team will help to drive the progress and attitudes of the less positive members.

Most people, as we have discussed previously, have a fear of change. It is a fear of the unknown and also a reluctance to move from a comfortable situation towards one that may not be quite so comfortable. This can be a particular problem if the organisation is successful and profitable – people will naturally feel, we're OK where we are, why fix something that isn't broken? But, as we have said, change is inevitable. It can't be avoided so we all have to learn to deal with it. So, overcoming a fear of change must be a priority at the start of any innovation. Communication is, as it often is, the key to success here. You will need to set up ways of getting the right messages out to all the members of your team and also give them the opportunity and encouragement to get their messages, fears and problems back to you. So, what do you need to let them know? Try this brief list:

- Set out your objectives for the change right from the start. State clearly what you want them to achieve – and why. You should use more than one method of doing this. Giving your message once will be effective in settling the fears of some team members, but not all. Plus, even these people may not take in all of your initial message. So, for example, you could call a team meeting and discuss future plans then follow this up with a written memo (perhaps sent by email) giving them all the same details. Of course, the tone of these communications should be positive and optimistic while being reassuring.

- Explain how dangerous it can be for an organisation to get too complacent. It is easy to think that you have a successful product range and don't need to change a thing but then the market changes and you are left behind.
- Acknowledge the risks of change but explain that not changing carries even greater risks. There are plenty of examples of how organisations who have refused to change have gone out of business.
- Point out that change will happen to us no matter what we do. Far better to make our own changes voluntarily and in a controlled manner than have them forced upon us.
- Draw on their experiences with customers. Ask them to evaluate whether all the customers that they come into contact with are 100 per cent satisfied. If, as is always the case, customers have complained or made suggestions about what they would really like, then that can be sufficient reason to change.

The second problem you may need to resolve is that of the disruptive team member. Having got a relatively hard-working, successful team up and running on a change project, you could find that there is one person who displays negative behaviour. They may continually avoid work or criticise management. This one person can easily 'poison' the attitudes of the whole team if not stopped. Some of this may be the result of fear that the individual feels but some people are naturally negative and will sabotage your efforts to change and to motivate your team if you do not deal with the problem. One way of trying to get this type of person onside is to ask their opinion on how to make things better. Trying to involve them more fully in the change programme and making them 'own' an idea is a good way to change their behaviour.

INSTANT TIP

Make sure that your team is given plenty of examples – stories of how other organisations have succeeded and also ones about how companies have failed because they did not change. Think of examples such as typewriter companies going out of business when they did not change to producing word processors.

The important thing to remember is that behaviour that is not helping the change – whether it be through fear or vindictiveness – cannot be allowed to derail the process. It must be dealt with in whatever ways are necessary.

Dealing with stress

Too much stress can be very damaging and all employers have a duty to protect their employees from undue stress as it can lead to serious illness. Any stress can in fact be detrimental in that it can lead to poor decision making and absenteeism, so it is in everyone's interests to avoid it. It will be useful at this point to give a brief definition of stress. The Health & Safety Executive define it as 'the adverse reaction people have to excessive pressure or other types of demand placed on them'. We have all been under pressure from time to time – pressure to meet a deadline or to get to an appointment on time, to revise for an exam, to achieve targets or to improve our performance at work. The consequences of too much pressure, which leads to stress, include:

- health problems – these can include exhaustion, heart conditions, burn-out, and high blood pressure

- increased absenteeism
- depression
- lower productivity
- decreased motivation.

However, some stress is inherent in most workplaces so what can be done to manage it? Human resources policies and occupational health schemes can help to recognise and treat stress and also put in place practices and systems that can help to prevent it occurring. Let's look at the possible causes of stress at work:

- conflict in the workplace
- bullying and harassment
- too few staff to cope with the workload
- lack of information and communication
- poor work–life balance
- long hours
- change
- boredom
- pressure to achieve improvements.

In terms of managing change, the possibility of stress must be taken into account during the planning and implementation of any change programme. Projects can be designed so that undue stress is taken into account and there are six areas where senior managers should pay particular attention:

1. Demands – when designing change programmes, the workload of each member of the team must be taken into account, along with the working hours, work patterns and the team's work environment. It is a manager's job to match the demands made upon each team member and the responsibilities they are given to their skills and abilities. Making unreasonable demands on a worker is one of the prime causes of stress in the workplace so a

manager needs to know the workers. Asking too much can be counter productive.

2. Change – many people find it difficult to cope with change and constant change that is not well managed and where the reasons for the change are not communicated properly can cause stress. Even small changes can be stressful so care must be taken to manage the communications around the situation and to ensure that workers are coping well.

3. Control – change can cause workers to feel out of control and this in turn will cause stress. Of course, a manager's job is to manage, but they must also make employees feel that they have a reasonable degree of control over their work situations.

4. Role – understanding their role and what is required of them is vital for an employee in order to avoid undue stress that will cause health problems. Again, communication is key. A manager must ensure that all team members fully understand what they have to do. The uncertainty that surrounds a badly defined work role can cause stress and fear, so clear role definitions and good communication about expectations is vital.

5. Support – even very difficult, pressurised work situations can be made less stressful by the right support system. Managers in organisations must put this system in place for all their workers so that they have team structures that help them to cope with the workload, the right resources to do the job that is asked of them and plenty of support from their line manager and colleagues.

6. Relationships – management must promote good working relationships with respect and consideration being afforded to all employees. If there is bullying or harassment in any area of the organisation it is management's responsibility to deal with it and to protect the employee concerned so that undue stress is avoided.

What this all amounts to is that organisations have a clear responsibility to look after their employees' well-being in relation to stress. Demands made on employees must be reasonable and tailored to individual employees and management must put in place the appropriate communication and support systems. Although the emphasis here has been on avoiding stress in order to protect the health and well-being of workers, there are benefits for organisations in ensuring that stress is kept to a minimum in the workplace. If stress can be controlled then productivity will be increased and the motivation of the workforce will be correspondingly higher, leading to a better retention of staff and lower sickness absence.

Recognising achievement

Whenever people have done well then their achievements should be recognised. There is a theory of 'positive reinforcement' that says that if good performance is rewarded it will be repeated and that is, of course, a desirable result of recognising achievement, but it is not the only benefit. There is a noticeable improvement in performance throughout an organisation when achievements are recognised and rewarded. This could be attributed to the 'feel good' effect of any reward scheme. If people feel that their efforts are being noticed then they will invariably work harder. This seems like a win-win situation, so that all organisations should implement a programme of rewards leading to inevitable success. But this is not the case. In some organisations, rewards and bonus schemes have been put in place that have had detrimental effects on the performance of individuals and of the organisation as a whole. This is because it is easy to set up bonus schemes that reward the wrong behaviour and often difficult to focus on the behaviour that will produce the right sort of results for the organisation. Sometimes bonus schemes can be manipulated so that bonuses are paid without their having produced any benefit for the organisation.

However, there are a number of gains that an organisation may make as a result of an incentive scheme that is well thought out.

More motivated staff

If the workforce believes that it will be properly rewarded for performing well then it will work harder and more productively. Care must be taken to set the right goals and to make sure that everyone understands what is required. A badly set up and explained scheme will have the opposite to the desired effect and may well mean that some members of the workforce work more slowly or less productively if they do not believe that the targets set are achievable or if they do not think that the scheme is fairly set up. Similarly, staff morale and loyalty will be improved with a good incentive scheme.

Better focus

A good incentive scheme will focus the minds of both management and employees. By deciding and then disseminating what is important to the organisation and building the targets of the scheme on this, everyone will be aware of what is needed not just to earn a bonus but also to improve the results of the organisation.

Improved teamwork

Teamwork will improve as a result of a scheme aimed at making people work together to achieve a common goal that will benefit both team members and the organisation.

Increased productivity

Increasing productivity and performance are what the objectives of the scheme should be. Good behaviours that are rewarded will usually be repeated and improvements should become continuous.

Retention of good staff

Competent staff will usually stay where they feel appreciated and rewarded. A good incentive scheme will ensure that an organisation is competitive in the labour market without involving an across-the-board pay increase, so it will be more cost effective.

Easier recruitment

An incentive scheme will often make future recruitment easier. The organisation's reputation for recognising achievement will be enhanced by a good incentive scheme and therefore good quality applicants are likely to come forward when new staff are needed, attracted by the organisation's reputation.

Management's positive reputation

A scheme can reinforce management's attitude to performance. A good incentive scheme that is taken seriously by both staff and management helps to promote the idea of continuous improvement and shows that management is fully behind the efforts. The goals that are set as part of an incentive scheme will reinforce the workforce's understanding of what is required.

Rewarding performance

So, how should good performance be rewarded? There are two main types of monetary incentive:

1. Bonus schemes – these are often paid annually to the entire workforce or to a section of the workforce and can be based on results achieved such as sales or production figures. The main disadvantage of bonuses is that many workers will usually receive a standard bonus calculated on results achieved by a team or by the organisation and individual effort may not be directly rewarded.

2. Savings percentages – these are used to recognise innovative achievements that result in cost savings to the organisation. This is a type of scheme that is often used in a manufacturing situation where potential cost savings have been spotted. The disadvantage with this type of scheme is that it can be difficult to pinpoint the person or persons who should receive it. Savings from innovations are rarely the work of just one person but these schemes often reward the one person who came up with (or can lay claim to) the original idea. But, of course, all ideas need work to turn them into something that will result in savings so many people who may have worked hard to make the idea work may be ignored in this situation. Also, cost savings directly relating to a single action or idea can be difficult to isolate and measure.

Apart from formal monetary incentive schemes, there are a number of ways – some of them relatively inexpensive – of recognising and encouraging good performance including:

● gift vouchers for local stores
● tickets to the theatre or sporting events

- vouchers for a meal at a local restaurant
- a gift such as a television
- a trip abroad
- a special awards ceremony
- a break at a luxury hotel.

Most managers will be able to come up with many more of this type of incentive and will be able to tailor them to the workforce, local circumstances and, of course, the budget available. The main advantage of this sort of incentive, apart from the low cost, is that it can be given quickly so that the reward can be closely linked to the good performance. With bonus schemes and schemes that pay a percentage of improvement savings there is an inevitable delay in getting the reward calculated and out to the workforce or to the person directly responsible for the savings, and this delay tends to dilute the motivational effect of the scheme.

While bonuses and incentive schemes are a popular way of recognising and encouraging good performance and innovation, they are not the only way. An extremely effective way of marking achievement is to simply make a fuss. Publicise the success both internally and externally. This can be done in a number of ways:

- in the company newsletter
- on internal notice boards
- on the organisation's website
- in the trade press
- in the local press
- on the company's intranet.

In general, people do like to see their name in print and this sort of action following a success sends a message to a number of different audiences. It tells the employee's colleagues about the good performance and will encourage them to try to emulate the success. It informs potential applicants for jobs in the organisation that there is a culture of improvement and of recognition of that improvement. It also tells competitors that the organisation is having some success. Recognition is a good motivator and will create a good impression with the workforce and with the wider public.

When designing an incentive scheme of any type the following should be taken into account.

Objectives

Be clear about the objectives of the scheme. In addition to improving profitability and productivity, many organisations use incentive schemes to retain staff or to encourage the recruitment of top quality new staff or to build stronger teams. Set clear goals and make sure everyone involved understands the performance criteria.

Look at your competitors

Check out what other organisations in your business area and locality are offering. You must make it competitive. This will ensure that the current workforce is satisfied and also that future employees will be attracted by the scheme.

Consultation

Make sure the scheme is seen as a real incentive by the people it is aimed at. The best schemes are usually the result of extensive consultation with staff and, where applicable, unions.

Payment intervals

Consider having scheduled payouts at relatively short intervals. A big payout once a year will not necessarily motivate and reward staff as effectively as quarterly or monthly targets and payouts. It can be difficult for a team to keep working towards a goal that is a long way off.

Limit the scheme's membership

Limit the number of different areas that the organisation is including in the incentive scheme. There are lots of areas that can be successfully incentivised but do not be tempted to try them all at once. Choose what is important for the business and that can be clearly measured. This may include a selection from customer retention, customer satisfaction, output per person, profit targets, quality-related targets, innovative projects and so on, depending on the priorities of the business.

Measure and monitor

Plan how you will measure the results and make the results known to every member of the team as you go along. Obviously there will be some element of surprise as to the exact payout at the last minute but people should always know if their current performance is good enough to earn the extra rewards. That is the point of incentive schemes.

Keep it on track

Make sure that you highlight areas where there are deficiencies while working towards the goals set by the scheme – by way of regular reviews – and that there is an opportunity to put things back on track with extra effort. Being seen to support staff in pursuit of an incentive payment is important.

Consider a scale of payments

Consider having a scale of payments so that progress towards the ultimate goal can be recognised with interim payments or with a scale of payments at the end of the bonus period according to how close to the goal employees have got rather than taking an 'all or nothing' approach.

Make it flexible

The scheme should meet the current needs of the business and also be suitable for adjustment so that future requirements can be taken into account. A scheme that can be changed from time to time has the extra benefit of keeping staff interested and motivated to work towards different goals to suit the business.

Use personalised goals

Try to incorporate personal goals for all individual team members in addition to the organisational objectives such as improved profitability and so on. Encouraging teamwork by having a corporate goal can be very successful in making sure that everyone works in the same direction but having their own personal goal can be very motivating to individuals and bring great benefits to an organisation.

Start small

It can be useful to try the scheme out on a small scale or over a limited time period before implementing it company-wide. Check the effectiveness of the scheme at the end of such a pilot scheme.

And finally, keep it simple.

Case study

A small manufacturing company decided to implement an incentive scheme with the aim of increasing profitability. Following extensive staff consultation – including anonymous surveys sent to every member of staff, several team meetings to generate ideas and get staff input and a review of what the business needed to move it forward – they came up with two objectives of the scheme:

1. to motivate staff
2. to increase profit by 10 per cent in the next year.

It was decided to incorporate both team goals and personal goals into the scheme and these were broken down into quarterly targets for each team and individual. The company felt that the individual goals would motivate staff while the team goals would foster better teamwork and the quarterly targets allowed them the flexibility that the business needed.

(Continued)

(Continued)

The profitability targets took into account three different measurements – revenue, profit margins and cashflow – so that different departments could contribute to the targets and the results were objective and easy to measure and understand. The scheme was set up so that individuals had their own targets based on their work roles. For example, accounts office workers were targeted on money being collected on time, sales people were given targets linked to revenue and production staff had targets based on profit margins so that wastage was controlled and costs kept down.

At the launch of the scheme meetings were held with staff in all departments to ensure that they fully understood the scheme and knew exactly what they had to do to earn a payment. Written details of the scheme were also sent to every member of staff. The scheme included payments on a sliding scale that allowed workers to earn a bonus even if they did not fully meet their targets but had made some progress.

When the scheme was launched managers set up monthly meetings to review progress towards both team goals and individual targets and made it clear that they were there to help.

At the end of the first quarter a major review of the scheme's success was carried out by the management team and the staff were also consulted. Although the ambitious profitability target had not been fully met, the majority of scheme members had earned incentive payments, and a staff survey revealed that a general increase in feelings of motivation and significant progress towards the profitability goal had been made. It was therefore decided to continue with the scheme with minor adjustments to the way results were measured. The management team felt that it would be able to concentrate on other issues such as customer satisfaction and new product launches in the future when it had established and improved the new profitability targets.

INSTANT TIP

Consult the people involved when you are setting up an incentive scheme. The people whose performance will be measured must believe in the scheme and they will know very well just what they consider to be an incentive.

In addition to incentive schemes, where specific targets are set and rewards are given for meeting them, an organisation can offer perks to attract and retain staff. Perks are things, such as private health cover, that can be given in addition to salary as part of a pay package. Items that could be offered as perks include:

- Private health cover – this can have extra benefits for an organisation in that employees may be able to plan when to receive treatment or absences may be reduced.
- Company cars – these are usually offered to employees who need to travel in the course of business and will attract a tax liability for the employee.
- Expenses – this could be for travelling or meals during the working day.
- Pensions – a generous pension scheme can be an important incentive for many workers but is becoming increasingly more expensive for an organisation to provide.
- Share option schemes – these allow employees to buy shares at favourable rates and there are tax benefits to be gained.
- Flexible working – this can attract good workers to an organisation.
- Gym membership – this can also have extra benefits for the organisation as staff will generally become fitter.

- Enhanced holiday entitlements – longer holidays can attract applicants when new staff are needed and can also be beneficial for existing staff.
- Training – an organisation that has a reputation for training its employees at all levels will always find staff recruitment and retention easier.

INSTANT TIP

Most incentives and perks have tax implications – financial rewards will usually be taxed and non-financial perks will have a tax liability for the employee if they have an equivalent cash value, so they must have a value to the employee that outweighs the tax they may have to pay on them.

As always, with any new initiatives that are introduced, comprehensive and ongoing evaluation is essential. In the case of incentive schemes, consider the following:

- Consult with the people involved. Did it motivate them? Did they feel it worked for them and for the organisation? Did they fully understand the scheme?
- Did it work for the organisation? The results that have been produced during the operation of the scheme must be compared with the original targets and with the overall cost of the scheme. Was it worth it?
- Was the scheme easy to operate? Are the details that are needed to calculate the payouts easily available?
- Is more training for staff needed to assist them in achieving their targets – either in explaining the scheme or giving them more tools to do their jobs better?
- Does the scheme need adjustment to make it work better in future? Should different areas of the business be

targeted, for example, or the scheme broadened out to include other departments?

● Has the organisation gained other benefits in addition to the easily-quantifiable results? For example, staff motivation and retention etc.

Whatever incentive scheme is introduced, bonuses agreed or perks offered, they should be given alongside a good pay structure. If staff are poorly rewarded in terms of their monthly salary, no incentives will make up for this and the result will be de-motivated staff and good staff leaving to seek better salaries elsewhere. Also, rewards will not make up for a poor management situation with a lack of communication and proper appraisals. Incentives and perks are no substitute for an attractive pay scheme and a well-managed organisation.

SUMMARY

This chapter examined why there is often opposition to change. We looked at the psychology of change and how people's emotions can be affected.

We then discussed how to overcome barriers to change including operational barriers such as tradition, location, technology, systems and the effects of past success or failure. The other set of barriers – related to how people feel – included fear, lack of understanding, insecurity, hanging on to familiarity and the effects of office politics. The main way of overcoming all these barriers is by way of good communication so we looked briefly at the principles of effective communication such as making things easy to understand, and making it brief, positive and direct.

Where office politics has the potential to damage an organisation or its change programme it must be dealt with. This can be done by encouraging competition and social

(Continued)

(Continued)

activities among teams and between departments, and by planning inter-departmental projects.

We saw that behaviour can be changed by – as always – communicating, and by building trust and cooperation, and by developing a cohesive team. This was followed by a list of things which, if communicated well, can overcome the fear of change. This included clearly stating objectives, explaining the risks that not changing can bring and asking for input from the workforce.

Next we looked at how to deal with stress. It can lead to lower productivity, poor decision making and absenteeism (and can cause serious illness) and is often caused by conflict, bullying, overwork, lack of communication and change. When planning change, managers should pay attention to workloads, communication, employees' understanding of what is required of them and relationships in the workplace.

Recognising achievement can improve performance so next we examined incentive schemes. Gains that these schemes can produce include motivating staff, improving teamwork and increasing productivity, and can also help to make staff retention and recruitment easier. We looked at two main types of incentive scheme – bonus schemes and savings percentages – as well as several ideas for relatively inexpensive ways of encouraging improved performance. Another way of recognising achievement is to publicise it in communications such as a company newsletter or the local and trade press.

Next we examined what to take into account when setting up an incentive scheme. Particular attention should be paid to the objectives set, competitor activity, measuring and monitoring results and consulting staff involved for their input.

ACTION CHECKLIST

1. How do you feel about change – excited, optimistic, afraid, pessimistic, cautious?
2. Which of the barriers to change mentioned above do you think is the most difficult to overcome?
3. Consider the methods of communication used in your own organisation? Are they used to best effect? Can you pinpoint areas for improvement?
4. Do you have personal experience of stress? How important do you think a work–life balance is in avoiding or overcoming stress?
5. Have you ever been involved in an incentive scheme? If so, did it have the desired effect? Did everyone involved have a proper understanding of it and what was required of them?

08

How will you know if the change has worked?

There is little point in spending great amounts of time and money to change something if it cannot be demonstrated that the process has produced the desired result. The key to this is in setting goals and objectives and putting in place systems right from the start that check progress against these goals.

Key management challenges in assessing change

Systems for assessing outcomes and monitoring change must be put in place in the initial stages of a change programme. They must form an integral part of the planning process and not be added as an afterthought to check if something has worked. In major change programmes in particular it is essential to plan in checks at regular intervals. Ideally this should involve senior management but in any event there should be someone designated to monitor progress along the way. This person – or persons – should have a sharp eye and great attention to detail, an ability to keep track of large quantities of data – possibly on a daily basis – and be capable of holding regular meetings to measure the results against the milestones that will have been planned into the change programme. Regular review meetings not only show how the programme's actual results to date compare with the projected figures but they can also be a forum for discussing successes to celebrate and problems to resolve along the way.

A further challenge is in dealing with problems as they arise. With systems in place from the start to check on progress against the project's objectives, it is essential to deal with issues immediately.

Monitoring systems

There are two aspects to consider when implementing systems to monitor results. One relates to what should be monitored and the other to how it should be monitored. In terms of what should be monitored, the following should be considered, according to the requirements of the change programme:

- customer records – details of orders placed, prices, deliveries, payments, who and where they are and so on
- records for potential customers – including what contact has been made
- supplier records – similar to the details held about customers
- employee details – contracts, terms and conditions, policies and procedures, attendance records and so on
- quality management records
- financial reports.

As an organisation grows, it is important to ensure that the right IT systems are in place to manage the vast amounts of information that will be generated. A review of the enormous variety of management information systems that are available is outside the scope of this book, but there are a few things to look for when choosing one that will be right for your organisation. When designing monitoring systems, it is always useful to incorporate, right from the start, mechanisms to put corrective action into place as well as to check whether a change has worked. The following criteria should be included in a system to check the effectiveness of a change programme:

- Quantifiable targets – knowing exactly what you were aiming at in terms of results is essential.
- Budget – how much time, employee-hours and money have been expended during the change programme and how does this compare with what was forecasted?
- Timeliness – has the project been brought in on time?
- Quality – how has the change impacted on the quality of goods and services that the organisation produces?
- Regular reports – was frequent feedback received during the life of the change programme?
- What corrective action has been taken during the project?
- How have customers responded to the changes made?
- How have relationships – both internal and external – worked during the change? Are changes to working relationships needed to facilitate the changes?

Monitoring systems should keep a check on the progress towards the goals of the change programme and not merely be a reporting system. As stated previously, these systems should incorporate mechanisms for putting right aspects of the change programme that are not working as intended and to ensure that the project is kept on track. These could take the form of regular meetings where results are presented and discussed with remedial action decided upon at the same meeting. They will probably also include regular reports bringing everyone – including stakeholders – up to date as to how the change is progressing. In the initial planning stages of any change programme it is essential to include a number of milestones with the results expected up to that date so that successes or failures become obvious as each milestone is reached. Examples of areas to monitor are outlined below.

Milestones

Milestones are key to a successful change programme. Key stages with measurable results should be identified at the planning stage and planned in so that progress can be monitored on a regular basis and the programme can be controlled and managed. Many tasks can be designated as milestones – even something as simple as completion of an inventory or a report being completed. The idea is that a milestone is a point at which it is possible to check that the programme is on schedule and not falling behind.

Progress

It may be desirable to monitor progress in terms of feedback from team members at regular meetings. The reported progress of a team member should be viewed in conjunction with the manager's observations as it is not good practice to rely simply on a team member reporting on their own progress. It is important to remember that until a task is completed, progress can be subjective. The only objective status judgements are 'not started' or 'completed'.

Duration of tasks

If, for example, setting up a particular system included in the change programme is allowed three weeks in the original plan, then any deviation from this will need to be noted and adjustments to the plan made accordingly. Gains in terms of less time spent on a task will inevitably be countered by losses when more time than had been allowed is used up. The problem arises when a task takes longer than planned and other tasks following immediately after are dependent on the results of the delayed task. Here, the team leader or senior manager's skills will be needed to make the necessary adjustments to the plan and to ensure that the change is not severely affected by the delay. There is more about planning later in this section.

Accomplishments

Where success is quantifiable at stages throughout the process it should be possible to monitor those successes and to celebrate them during the process. This not only provides another monitoring point, it also gives an opportunity to mark success and motivate the entire team.

Use of resources

Careful control of resources such as finances, equipment and employee hours is essential. Many stakeholders would consider a change programme unsuccessful if the budget for these items was exceeded, no matter what results were achieved in terms of improved performance. All resources used should be recorded and compared against what had been planned for at that point in the process.

The Gantt chart

A useful tool in monitoring results and targets during the life of a change programme is the Gantt chart. This is a type of bar chart that shows, in graphic form, the different stages of the programme. A chart like this illustrates the start and finish dates of each element of the change programme and can be used throughout the programme to show the progress that has been made by using percentage shading of each element to show how much has been completed and also by the addition of a 'today' line that will highlight the point that has been reached. A Gantt chart will also show which parts of the programme overlap and which must be completed before another stage can commence. This type of planning tool must be used after all the tasks have been listed. Gantt charts can be prepared using easily available software. Look at the example shown in Figure 8.1.

A Gantt chart is usually prepared by entering details of tasks into the relevant software package. One thing to take particular care about is the dependency and timing of the various work elements. It is tempting to try to shorten the change programme by allowing a second stage to commence before another is completed when in reality it relies on results from this preceding stage so extra care should be taken at this point. Remember that what you produce on a complicated-looking chart will not change reality. The work still has to be done and it will be done a great deal more efficiently if this planning stage is completed honestly, realistically and comprehensively. Short cuts or deceiving oneself at this stage will only result in a poorly run change programme.

SCHEDULE

Calendar weeks			1	2	3	4	5	6	7	8	9	10
Week commencing	Employee days allocated	Who allocated	20-Apr	27-Apr	04-May	11-May	18-May	25-May	01-Jun	08-Jun	15-Jun	22-Jun
ACTIVITY												
Meet stakeholders and gain agreement on activities and timescales												
Review entry criteria for course												
Identify outcome evidence required to evaluate service												
Identify information requirements:												
Course data												
Setting of interviews with course deliverers												
Request and chase key data												
Development of questionnaires for:												
Service providers												
Staff												
Setting/aligning of interviews												
One-to-one interviews												
Review of interviews, identification of commonalities												
Preparation of report												
Interviews with attendees – what worked, etc.												
Interviews with staff, key stakeholders, including commissioners												
Review of key interviews and collation of key issues												
Quantitative analysis of current service provision/outcomes												
Review												
Delivery of final report/presentation												
Weekly review meetings (internal)												
Fortnightly email updates												
Monthly report												
Major reviews												

Figure 8.1 Example Gantt chart

Short- and long-term gains

Every change programme will be aiming to improve something in the organisation, whether it be greater efficiency, decreased costs, increased profits or something entirely different. They will have goals and objectives to achieve. Quite often these goals and objectives are concentrated right at the end of the programme. After months of hard work the results will be assessed and it will be decided whether or not the goals have been achieved. For example, current costs will be compared with what had previously been paid or the results of a customer survey completed prior to the change with a new customer survey after the programme has been completed. The programme will be wrapped up, everyone involved will be congratulated – or not, if the change has not been completely successful! – and all will go back to their old jobs or on to the next change. However, if the change programme takes months to complete there is a danger that people will lose sight of the ultimate goal and may become de-motivated or lose direction. It is therefore useful to plan short-term gains throughout the life of the programme. This could be, for example in a production method change, staged improvements. By the end of the first month a change could have been made that reduces waste, by the end of the third month an improvement in throughput could be aimed at, and by the end of a six-month change programme, for example, the cost savings and increased productivity could be fully reported.

The long-term gains are more obvious. When deciding the scope of the changes at the initial planning stages, the main goals and objectives are usually the impetus for the change and will shape the programme. However, it is worth giving considerable thought to all the gains that are possible in the long term, while focusing on the primary outcome. The ultimate goal of any change programme will be the driver of the change so it is likely to be something like 'increase profitability' or 'improve efficiency', specified in quantifiable terms. However, how you achieve the goal – the objectives – will bring a variety of gains in the long term. If we take, for example, the goal of increasing profit then this could be done by developing a new product. If successful and managed correctly, the gains that could come from this include:

- Increased profit – this is the obvious one as it's almost always the reason for the change programme.
- Improved customer service – when a profitable new product is successfully launched, it is important to announce it to customers, concentrating on how it improves what the organisation is offering and pointing out the benefits to customers. If customer comments and surveys have had an input into the product development process this should be pointed out, thereby making the point that the organisation is responsive to customer requirements.
- Increased competitiveness – a successful new product will keep the organisation's product offering competitive, especially if it is ahead of other things on the market.
- Raised share price – in the case of a major product launch for a public company the share value may be positively affected.
- Kudos – taking part in a successful change programme can improve the reputation of both the team leader and all members of the team.
- Future changes – many change programmes uncover other areas that need improvement and a successful team may go on to take part in other change programmes.
- Experience – again, this is something that will be a gain for the change team and ultimately for the organisation's benefit.

As you can see, the benefits of a successful change programme are many and varied. They do not always accrue just to the organisation as the team and its leader can also gain. The gains that are made on behalf of the organisation should be listed and explained in the closing report of the programme.

Assessing the outcomes of your plans

One of the most common questions asked after a change programme will be 'Was it successful?' If the goal of the change was something simple, quantifiable and well-defined the answer could be a straightforward 'Yes', but changes in organisations are rarely that simple. There will be lots of things to take into account such as the effect on customers, suppliers, other departments, efficiency and so on. Obviously, these are more difficult to measure in that they are not quantitative and any assessment is necessarily based on comparative methods. However, it is usually possible to find a quantitative way of measuring even qualitative aspects of the change. For example, customer satisfaction could be measured by comparing the number of complaints received per month before the change programme was carried out with the number received after the improvements. Alternatively the effect on cooperation between departments could be measured by use of a questionnaire.

Of course, not only the planned outcomes of a change programme should be assessed. There may be effects on the organisation that were not envisaged and these should also be noted and evaluated. A change in one department may have knock-on effects for one other related department or for the whole organisation. Also, effects on areas outside the organisation should be taken into account. For example, have any environmental changes been made (waste or emissions increased or reduced)? Or maybe competitors or suppliers will have been affected by your changes. For this reason, as well as the need for information on the outcomes of the change, a thorough review of all the effects must be carried out.

So, to summarise, in assessing the outcomes of a change programme the following questions must be answered:

- What were the quantified results?
- Which parts worked?
- Which parts did not work?
- What further action is necessary?
- What have been people's reactions?
- What have we learned?
- Who else has been affected?
- What else needs to be done?

Acting on assessments

As always, whenever assessments are carried out the results of the assessment must be acted upon. This applies particularly if some of the results are unexpected. Also, a wide-ranging review of the change programme may well throw up some aspects that will point an organisation to further changes that are necessary or lessons that can be learned for the future.

If people are to be convinced as to the success of a change programme they will need to see evidence. If possible, a full report detailing the effects of the programme should be circulated or made available to all employees and other interested parties. There may be some aspects of the process that are confidential – sales or profit figures, for example – so, although a full report will need to be prepared for stakeholders and senior management, it will be necessary to inform others about the success of the changes in an abbreviated format. It may be possible to use the main report as a basis for this and perhaps, for example, amend the confidential parts by using percentages rather than actual figures and by cutting out some of the more detailed passages. It is useful to include a section on why the changes were deemed necessary and a summary of the changes made.

For the full effects of a successful change programme to be achieved the changes will need to be embedded into the organisation. This can be difficult as there is a natural tendency to slip back into old ways. There may have been training needs identified during the change programme as people may have been unable to cope fully with the new systems that have been introduced. Obviously, these needs must be satisfied as soon as possible to avoid losing the gains that have been made as a result of the change. The change programme may have other effects that must be dealt with to ensure its continuing success. These would include possible changes that have become necessary to pay arrangements – for example, if someone has had to take on duties that attract a higher level of pay – or teams may need to be changed as a result of how the changes have affected people's workloads or if there have been promotions and so on.

Finally, there will be a need to recognise achievements made by the change team as a whole and by individuals involved. Publicising success in this way is an ideal way of drawing attention to achievements, motivating the people concerned and convincing everyone in the organisation – and beyond – that real changes have been successfully made.

INSTANT TIP

Keep communication about the changes going even after the end of a specific change programme. This will help to ensure that the change has permanent rather than temporary effects.

Providing constructive feedback

The aim of any feedback must be the improvement of performance. Positive feedback will usually also have the benefit of providing encouragement and support to team members. However, it is sometimes necessary to provide what could be viewed as negative feedback, i.e. when something is not being done as required or as well as could be expected and this is often termed 'constructive feedback'. Let's look at the two types of feedback.

Positive feedback

This has a number of positive effects for the person receiving it and for the team as a whole. These include raising the morale of both the individual team member and the team as a whole, encouraging the behaviour that is required, facilitating the coaching of team members and increasing the recipient's confidence.

Constructive feedback

The main aim of this type of feedback is to change behaviour and there are several things to take into consideration when delivering it. First, it is important to find the right time and place to give constructive feedback as it can produce a negative reaction. Delivering any feedback that could be viewed as critical should always be done in private. If people feel attacked they could react in a number of ways, perhaps drawing attention to something which would be better kept private. (Note that although positive feedback is far less likely to produce a negative reaction, it should usually be delivered in private – the right time and place – and kept to specific matters. The only exception to this is when the feedback can be used as public recognition when, of course, attention should be drawn to the behaviour that attracted the feedback.) Second, the feedback should focus on behaviour rather than on anything personal. For this reason what is said should be specific as general comments can be perceived as a personal attack.

INSTANT TIP

When delivering constructive feedback it is best to avoid the use of very general words such as 'never' and 'always' as these can produce a negative reaction: for example, saying 'you never finish a task' or 'you are always late' are unlikely to be completely true and will not be well received or help to solve the problem.

The third point that should be noted when giving constructive feedback is that the person receiving the feedback must be given time to consider the comments and to reply if they want to. Many managers will feel uncomfortable if they are delivering comments that could be viewed as criticism and may talk too much. The best thing to do is to state the case simply and then pause, giving the recipient a chance to respond. Remember that the aim of the process is to improve behaviour so it is important to try not to aggravate the person and to work towards a mutually acceptable solution. Giving constructive feedback is often an opportunity to coach a team member and one way of doing this is to lead the person towards a solution by asking questions and letting them feel that they have come up with the solution.

Feedback – whether of the kind that praises a team member or constructive feedback – is always a positive force in a team and is far preferable to no feedback being delivered, so long as it is aimed at achieving change and done in the right way.

SUMMARY

This chapter focused on how to check if the change programme has worked and achieved the results that were planned. We looked at the importance of putting systems in place in the initial stages of the change. These monitoring systems should include checks to show that the programme is on time, on budget and on target, that corrective action has been carried out and also make checks on its impact on customers. Keeping things on time and in sequence is particularly important and we looked at how Gantt charts could help with this.

We then examined the short- and long-term gains that could be achieved by a change programme. Short-term gains achieved throughout the programme can have a motivating effect whereas long-term gains are the focus of a change programme and include increased profitability, competitiveness and share prices, plus improved customer service. There are also benefits to team members carrying out a successful change programme including enhancing their reputation and experience.

Assessing outcomes was also examined. This is an important part of any change programme and can be done by comparing results before the change with those achieved after the change has been completed. As discussed, almost all aspects of an organisation can be measured numerically and then compared easily to assess the effectiveness of the change programme.

Finally we looked at the two types of feedback – positive feedback that usually takes the form of praise and constructive feedback, which is aimed at changing behaviour.

ACTION CHECKLIST

1. Consider how you would monitor the impact of changes on customers.
2. Prepare a simple Gantt chart to monitor your work plans for the next two days.
3. Think of three examples of short-terms gains that could be made during the life of a change programme.
4. Have you ever benefited from taking part in a change programme? If so, how, and how long did the effect last?
5. Think of an example of behaviour that could be changed using constructive feedback.

09

Do you have to abandon current methods?

Although, as we have discussed, change is constant and organisations will need to be always striving for improvement if they are to become, or remain, profitable, it is not usually necessary to throw out everything that is currently being done. A major part of a manager's skill lies in deciding exactly what requires radical change, what requires minor adjustment and what should be maintained.

Change and continuity

In deciding what to change and what to leave alone, a manager will need to conduct thorough reviews of the organisation including examining the strategy for the business and how all the various areas of it are performing. Improving performance is at the heart of any change.

As we all know, change is all around us. Society does not stay the same and the older ones among us will be amazed at the changes in, for example, technology or employment in our lifetimes. Organisations have to function – and thrive – in this rapidly changing environment. This does not mean that all the old ways of doing things have to be thrown out and everything re-invented, it simply means that in their quest for continuous improvement, managers must take account of the ever-changing environment. Old methods must be continually reviewed and if they still work and will allow the organisation to function and thrive in today's environment then they have earned their place and can stay, but if they no longer work or if better ways of doing things have been found then they will have to go. There is no room for sentiment or fear of change in business.

So, what has changed in the business and wider environment and how must organisations deal with these changes? The major changes that have taken place in the last few decades can be summarised as follows.

Technology

This is probably one of the most dramatic changes that has taken place in recent years. The pace of change in this area is extremely fast and it affects all industry sectors. This includes changes to our social, business and economic lives resulting in: jobs being redeployed or lost with the development of different industries while other industries disappear; telecommunications advances that have changed our daily lives (just think of emails and mobile phones that we hadn't even heard of just a few years ago but which are a major part of many people's lives now); and advances that have resulted in the globalisation of business.

People's expectations

Products and services are continually improving and being superseded by new products coming on to the market. This has led to people generally having higher expectations.

Global changes

There are constant changes in the political and economic situations in all areas of the world. Political changes in Eastern Europe have affected the employment situation in the United Kingdom, the ending of the Cold War with the Soviet Union (plus the political changes there) affected a number of industries including travel and armaments, and economic changes in China and India affect us all in terms of the goods we can buy in the shops.

Social changes

Demographic changes including increased life expectancy affect many organisations and the products and services they offer. From this change in society alone – and there have been many others – needs have changed dramatically. For example, there is now a demand for better healthcare, care in old age, new drugs are constantly being developed, housing needs have changed and demands for better leisure and travel opportunities have increased.

Environmental concerns

The need to look after the planet occupies the time of many organisations in a way it did not do just a few decades ago. New industries have sprung up that concentrate on areas allied to environmental concerns. Also, organisations are encouraged – and in some instances forced by regulations – to change how they work to reduce emissions and waste.

However, amid all this change all organisations need to achieve stability so that they can function long term as thriving businesses. Organisations must therefore be managed amid pressures for change resulting from the developments discussed above, including:

- Changing markets – with globalisation comes extra competition and new demands for different products.
- Changing competition – now, an organisation's main competitor may not be the similar-sized business just around the corner but a huge multi-national thousands of miles away which is able to serve its market just as well.
- Changing technology – this has changed the way businesses work, made communications with countries around the world easier and affected every area of business leading to expectations of super-fast responses and the ability to deal with enormous amounts of information.
- Changing work situations – production facilities or service industries (for example, call centres) can now be located anywhere in the world, putting pressure on businesses to increase efficiency and reduce costs in order to survive. Also, the workforce has become more mobile and more amenable to changing working patterns (think of Sunday trading, for example).

Regardless of all the changes going on in the world around them, organisations are always driven by the need to maximise profit and increase efficiency. They will have to achieve these aims by changing systems and structures within their organisations while also dealing with the changes in external conditions such as the economic and political developments as detailed above.

Assessing current methods

We have already discussed strategic planning at length, i.e. deciding where the business is now, where it should be in the future and how it will get there, but looking at current methods is slightly different. This is not aimed at developing a strategy for the organisation; its purpose is to look closely at exactly how the organisation is doing what it is doing. This sort of assessment could cover a wide variety of business aspects including how goods are produced, which suppliers are used, how many people it takes to do a job, how invoices are produced and credit control carried out, how staff rotas are worked out and even how stationery is ordered.

The people who should always be involved in this sort of assessment are the people doing the work. So, if you want to know how payments are currently being chased up, ask the staff in the credit control office. They will probably be happy to tell you – step-by-step. They will also have plenty of ideas on how to improve the process and will tell you just what are the problems caused by current methods and how to resolve them. Some of the ideas they come up with will inevitably be unrealistic. They may, for example, tell you that the only way to resolve the problems that crop up in their day-to-day working lives is by spending huge amounts of money on something that would not sufficiently benefit the organisation as a whole to justify the expenditure. But there will also be some good ideas produced.

As can be seen, this sort of assessment is so wide-ranging that it is inevitable that lots of ideas of what can be improved will be produced and we will now look at deciding what to do next.

How to decide which ideas to pursue

Deciding which of the ideas to pursue after conducting a thorough assessment of current ways of doing things can be a difficult task. One way of shortening the list of possibilities is to review each individual task, asking yourself whether it is important or urgent, or both, or neither, and then to deal with the task accordingly. So, using the urgent/important rule, the list of tasks will be dealt with as follows:

● If it is decided that something is urgent and important you need to do it immediately.
● If it is urgent but not important you can choose to delegate it or plan to do it yourself later.
● If a task is important but not urgent it can be planned into future activities.
● If it is decided that a task is neither important nor urgent then it doesn't need to be done.

These decisions about importance and urgency will help to prioritise work and to whittle down the seemingly impossible list of tasks that will be produced by a thorough overhaul of current methods used in a business. Good communication is essential when conducting this sort of exercise. Reassurance that not everything will change is important and, when changes are decided upon, an explanation of why they are necessary, how they will affect people and what they will achieve, along with extensive consultation and feedback, is essential.

Promoting the right culture for change

Many organisations pay lip service to innovation. It is often part of the mission statement or declared values of the business but then very little happens and nothing is done to encourage innovation among the workforce. But innovation and change, like all aspects of business, must be justified, so it is useful to make this a priority right from the outset. This establishing of the right culture for change must come from the top, so management's intentions should be firm and properly communicated to staff. This statement should not only assert that innovation will be encouraged but also be backed up with action and resources. This commitment can be shown in a number of ways, which we will look at in more detail in the next section on establishing strategies for change.

It will be useful to look now at just what 'culture' is. It can be seen as the way things are done and the system of values and beliefs that exists in an organisation. An organisation's culture can be very powerful in maintaining the status quo but for change to be successful that culture must change first. It will have become entrenched over time and will involve a variety of factors:

- The organisation's history – often an organisation will be set up in a particular period when a set of management methods are in vogue and then never change from that point in terms of culture. So, for example, a company might have been started in a period when authoritarian management was the current style and it may be difficult for the owners and managers of such a company to encourage more involvement from workers.
- The organisation's senior management or owners – their attitudes will have a great bearing on the culture of an organisation. Values come from the top and if senior managers are not receptive to change then major changes in the organisation's systems will be rare.

- The size of an organisation – if it is a small, owner-managed company then change will often be easier than if it is a large, multi-national, publicly-owned company. On the other hand, large companies usually have to answer to shareholders who may demand results. If change is the only way to get the results demanded then changes will have to be made.
- How creative the processes are that are at the centre of the organisation – some organisations are built upon straightforward production processes that carry on producing the goods without requiring constant change. Other organisations have to operate in a far more creative environment and will have to embrace change far more frequently. For example, a manufacturer of standard components will probably not change its manufacturing methods unless change is forced upon it by changing demands in its marketplace, whereas a design agency will conduct business in a far more experimental manner.

So, it can be seen from how an organisation's culture is established that it will be closely allied to its size, structure and stage of development, and will have to be a match for the market in which it operates. Any particular type of culture is not necessarily 'wrong' – it is just that some cultures embrace change more easily and if change becomes necessary and it is to happen, it may be that the culture has to change first depending on the type of culture in operation. For this reason it is essential that a manager leading a change programme understands the type of culture in operation. A thorough understanding of how the values and beliefs can impact upon what a manager does – or tries to do – is invaluable. Culture can affect a number of aspects of managing an organisation including:

- the strategy that is used to direct the organisation
- how the team is managed on a day-to-day basis

- how much autonomy team members have
- how members of the organisation react to change.

Change is about more than changing production methods or installing new technology and it is unlikely to happen if the right culture is not in place. Changing the culture of an organisation is not an easy task. It involves the value system of the organisation and ensuring that correct attitudes and beliefs are held throughout the organisation. Every action taken by management must echo the values so that they permeate the organisation. If a major change is attempted while the old values are still entrenched then failure will result as the new system or technology will be in place but there will be opposition to it and it will not work as intended. Changing attitudes involves dealing with barriers to change and this was discussed in detail in Chapter 7.

Establishing strategies for achieving change

As discussed above, the lead for change must come from the top and it is important for senior managers to do everything possible to make their commitment to change known to everyone in the organisation. With total commitment and back-up from management it is possible to change attitudes within an organisation and to promote a culture of innovation. This will involve:

- stating exactly why innovation is important to the organisation
- fostering a positive attitude – this involves, for example, asking positive rather than negative questions throughout the organisation (for example, asking what went right rather than what went wrong)

- recognising that what is currently in operation is not what is wanted and showing why things must change
- asking all employees to come forward with ideas to improve the organisation – and being positive about any ideas that are suggested. (It is important that no ideas are ruled out without proper consideration and that people are encouraged for simply coming up with ideas, i.e. the ideas don't have to be proved to be profitable before the employee is praised.)
- stating the commitment to take all suggestions seriously – to listen and respond appropriately
- encouraging creative behaviour throughout the organisation – this can be via managers reinforcing the sorts of things that they want to happen, i.e. the behaviours that will foster creativity such as risk taking, trying new ways of doing things and interdepartmental cooperation
- suggestions of where improvement may be possible and/or desirable
- committing resources – a statement that resources such as time and money plus any necessary training will be made available for all ideas that are accepted
- reassurance that failure will not be penalised – not every idea will work
- a promise that all ideas that do work and result in improvements will be rewarded
- setting up an easy to understand system whereby all ideas can be evaluated
- fostering team working by setting team goals and rewarding high performing teams – more about this in the next section.

Supporting your team

Teams work better than any other form of work structure and can perform well under most circumstances. However, they will not work properly if unsupported by people above and around them. A good team will achieve great results but a poor team will achieve very little and may even work to the detriment of the organisation. Teams can be beset by problems such as:

- Unclear goals – it is the team leader's and management's job to make sure the team know where it is going, what it is aiming at and why.
- Poor leadership – this can take the form of someone who leaves a team to its own devices too much, manifested by a lack of leadership or a leader who is too controlling so that the team members do not have any autonomy, i.e. the chance to affect the outcomes. There must be clear leadership so that every member of the team knows what they have to do and is helped and supported both by their fellow team members and the team leader.
- Lack of resources – this includes management time, training, sufficient team members, technology and tools. So, for example, if there are too few members of a team to carry out the amount of work they have to do or if they do not have the necessary skills within the team, then results will be poor. Resources such as the necessary training to create the right skills must also be readily available.
- People problems within the team – this can range from two or more team members simply not getting on with each other to a single disruptive member of the team or some team members not pulling their weight. Teams must be run so that the separate employees work as a team rather than allowing cliques to form or personality clashes to disrupt the team.

- Lack of support from outside the team – it is the team leader's job to ensure that the team gets the cooperation it needs from other departments.
- Poor communication – a team leader must ensure that teams have the systems and resources to communicate with each other and to receive communications from their leader, from senior management and from other departments.
- Lack of focus – a team leader should do just that – lead the team. They must be focused on their goals.

What's expected from a team leader?

So, what does a team expect and need from its team leader? The short answer is support, of course, but what does that entail? There are a number of aspects of a team leader's role that all come together to form the essential support that a team needs. This covers leadership, training, coaching, communication, provision of resources and being a link between the team and the rest of the organisation. Let's look at some of the aspects of a team leader's role that involve supporting the team.

The most important – and possibly widest – aspect of the role is that of leadership as this encompasses setting the direction and focus of a team as well as ensuring that it is motivated and managed on a daily basis. Without a clear focus the team will inevitably flounder. The team leader will need to create – with the team – performance goals that it must meet collectively and which are discussed and updated on a regular basis. Everyone in the team must be clear about their role and their goals. A good team leader will not impose standards, values and goals on a team but will collaborate with and guide the team to achieve good performance.

Training and coaching are an invaluable method of support that a team leader can bring to a team. Without the necessary skills not only will a team fail to achieve its goals but it will also be thoroughly miserable. Although a team leader's job is to achieve results through the team rather than worrying about keeping members happy, a team that is frustrated by a lack of results and feels that it is not supported will not achieve much.

Training is a very important resource that a team leader must assess the need for and then arrange so that the team does not suffer from a lack of skills. The training required may be technical skills connected to individual work roles or team skills that will help members work better together. Technical job skills could include anything specific to the job such as the use of technology, report writing or machine operation. Team skills will show team members how to work more productively together and could include how to conduct short but effective meetings, how to plan or run meetings, goal setting, decision making or problem solving as a group, or methods of group communication. This could take the form of formal, external training but is likely to be more effective if run as an internal workshop with the team involved working on teamwork exercises.

INSTANT TIP

Prompt provision of the right resources will ensure that the team can get on with its job. These resources include, as we have said previously, time, training, technology and tools.

Cross-training

A team leader should also pay attention to the team's needs for cross-training. This is where team members learn more about one another's work roles. Cross-training has a number of benefits for both the team and management:

- It promotes understanding between team members – the more they learn about other team roles the more they will appreciate the efforts of their colleagues and be able to help them in their roles in order to achieve their common goals.
- The team leader gains workers who may be almost interchangeable so that not only can they help each other with their work in busier times but can also cover for each other in the case of absence.
- Learning is often motivating in itself – being offered training can make people feel appreciated and valued and may offer them more security if they feel that they have become more useful to the organisation.
- It builds connections between team members.

Other aspects

The team leader's work role involves acting as a link between the team and the rest of the organisation and this can be a very important method of support for the team. If members of a work team feel that they are opposed – or at the very least not helped – by people outside the team but within the organisation then they need the team leader to put their case and help them to get the best deal possible so that the team has a good chance of success.

Finally, good communication is vital. With a group of people who have to work together, communication between them, between them and their team leader and between members and the rest of the organisation can make the crucial difference between success and failure. Regular meetings – kept short and well-planned – are an important part of keeping teams informed and on track. Teams must be told about any changes in their direction, the organisation's direction and progress, and kept in the picture about anything that will affect them. A lack of good communication leads to confusion and de-motivation.

SUMMARY

Here we looked at how organisations have to deal with continuing change to improve performance internally, at the same time as dealing with extensive changes externally, including technological, social and global changes, increasing environmental concerns and changes in people's expectations. Despite these changes organisations have to maintain stability in an effort to increase competitiveness and profitability in order to thrive in today's world while still holding on to the existing methods that work and changing what doesn't.

In assessing current methods, an organisation will need to examine how it is doing what it is doing. We discussed the importance of involving the people who do the actual work so that problems can be uncovered and resolved. The next step is to decide which ideas to pursue and, using the urgent/important rule, how to prioritise the implementation.

Next we looked at developing a culture for change and how culture is affected by many aspects of an organisation including its history, its management and/or owners, its size and how creative it is in general. Changing an organisation's culture can have an effect on an organisation's strategy, team management and how its workforce reacts to change. To develop a change culture, management must be committed to it and foster a positive attitude throughout the organisation by communicating thoroughly the reasons for change and encouraging creative behaviour.

Finally in this chapter we looked at how to support a team by the provision of adequate resources, training and cross-training (i.e. learning about one another's work roles), setting clear goals alongside excellent leadership and, above all, plenty of communication.

ACTION CHECKLIST

1. How have technological changes affected your work role in recent years?
2. What actions has your organisation had to take to protect the environment?
3. Take your 'to do list' for today and prioritise it according to the urgent/important rule.
4. Consider your organisation's culture. From what you know about it, what factors have had an effect on its development?
5. Is there someone on your level in your organisation whose work role you would like to learn more about? If so, find ways to go about this.

10

What are the costs of change?

The main reason for changing is usually to improve profitability. There may be other reasons stated such as improving efficiency, cutting costs, increasing customer satisfaction or satisfying shareholders and so on, but all of these can be summed up by saying they are aimed at improving the 'bottom line'. The methods may vary but the aim is the same. However, extra profits don't come free. To increase profit always requires hard work, time and other resources. Let's look at the costs of change.

Financial costs

Making changes in any organisation almost always costs money. New technology is often a major focus of a change programme and can be very costly. Although many changes will ultimately save the organisation money, in terms of decreased materials or running costs for example, there will usually have to be some initial financial investment in the health of the organisation for the future. These costs could include any of the following.

Redundancy

Redundancy payments may have to be made if the workforce is to be reduced.

INSTANT TIP

If redundancies become necessary it is vital that current legislation is complied with. This provides for consultation with staff and, where applicable, unions. Your local Chamber of Commerce, Business Link or trade association will be able to help you with this. Of course, if you work in a large organisation, your HR Department should lead this type of change.

Relocation

The cost of purchasing or renting new premises, legal fees and so on plus the costs of moving the production facilities will need to be accounted for if the organisation is to be relocated. There may also be compensation payments to the workforce or possibly extra travelling expenses paid for them for a period of time following the move.

Rebranding

If the organisation undergoes a change of name or logo there will be rebranding costs. This may involve the design and printing of new stationery, packaging and changing the old designs wherever they appear such as on delivery vans or advertising. This could occur when there is a change of ownership or when a whole product range is re-launched in an effort to revive its fortunes.

Communication

As always, communication is very important and some resources will have to be put into letting everyone know about the changes. This might include informing staff, announcing the changes – and the benefits – to customers and suppliers, and changing bank accounts in the case of a change of company name.

All of these financial costs will have to be taken into account when calculating whether or not the change will be a profitable one for the organisation. We will look next at costs that may not appear, at first, to be financial.

Case study

Relocation is costly in both financial terms and in the amount of stress and upheaval it generates. This case study tells the story of a manufacturer of small automotive parts who was finding that a lack of space in the factory was inhibiting its drive for growth. The first impulse was, of course, to look for larger premises but it carried out a full review of the business and its operations before taking a decision on when, where and whether to move. The manufacturer looked at all areas of the business rather than concentrating solely on the production area as it felt that if it were to make major changes then it must fully understand all the problems – and the advantages – that it had. Management assembled a team from all areas of the business and sent them on a one-day course held by a local consultant who helped them to examine the business and to see the possibilities that a change programme could offer.

A need for training was identified. The team's experience on the one-day course was very positive and made members realise that many in the organisation could benefit from training. They also realised that there was a lack of motivation among the production workers. *(Continued)*

(Continued)

The team's review also quickly confirmed management's conviction that the factory was currently incapable of producing more. However, team members were encouraged by what they had learned on the course about not making assumptions and examining every aspect of a situation. They knew the disadvantages of relocating were onerous as the expense of relocating machinery would be high, many staff would not be prepared to move and production would be disrupted for several weeks during the move, losing sales and possibly losing customers who would need to look for a continuous supply of the components. Also, the current factory was ideally situated as it was close to several of its largest customers and had a ready pool of experienced staff.

In view of all this, the team looked at various alternative solutions and finally recommended a reorganisation of the production area, with the workforce organised into teams responsible for their own area in terms of staff recruitment and training, cleanliness, delivery times and output. As the change programme progressed the people appointed as supervisors of these new production teams were brought in to the change team and given training about workflows and production throughput systems. They were then fully involved in devising the layout of their production areas, having been given a 'clean sheet' by the senior managers. Simple changes to systems were devised and introduced and workflows and outputs improved by 25 per cent within weeks of the new layouts becoming operational. By splitting the production area into separate areas with each one managed by a different team, customer service was not compromised.

Although surprised that relocation was not necessary, the senior managers were satisfied with the outcome as the costs of the training and other changes were far less than the costs of moving would have been and, in addition, they had a far more motivated and better trained group of production workers.

Valuable lessons

This case study provides a number of valuable lessons for anyone looking at changing an organisation:

- Don't make assumptions – no matter how obvious the need for change appears to be, do the work to evaluate the situation.
- A thorough review of the business will usually present opportunities.
- Successful change demands commitment from the top.
- Training can produce surprising results.
- Outside help is sometimes necessary. It can be difficult to see problems and issues that you are very close to.
- Involving staff is essential. Getting the people who have to do the work to feel that they own the change will dramatically increase the chances of success.
- Try not to hang on to old work methods – keep an open mind as to the possibility that there might be a better way to do something.

Costs of change involve more than money

As we said earlier, changing anything in any organisation will always incur costs. Most of these costs, such as those detailed above, will usually be quantifiable in terms of money. Even if the main input to the change has been someone's time and effort, this can be given a monetary value in terms of their hourly or monthly rate of pay. If machinery has to be moved to facilitate a production change, new technology installed to change an accounting system or staff given extra training to be able to deal with a new system, for example, this can also be calculated and given a financial value.

Even if sales temporarily dip because of breaks in supply or other problems caused by changes, this again can be quantified. There are, however, some effects of changes that cannot be reduced to money terms.

Stress

As we discussed in previous chapters, many people resist change and will find it stressful. Even people who do not have to carry out any of the work associated with the change may suffer from stress. This is usually because of the insecurity generated during any change process. Even the threat of change can be stressful to many workers. They will fear job losses or major changes to their work role with duties that they are afraid they will not be able to cope with.

The way to combat this fear – and thereby reduce the stress suffered within the organisation – is to communicate. As Sir John Tusa (see Chapter 12) points out, often people will see the start of changes and fear that redundancies will be widespread and so continuing with further changes will, in his words, 'need some careful footwork' – in other words, precise communication. Extensive programmes of team meetings, newsletters, workshops, individual meetings, emails and general notices can be put in place so that everyone in the organisation is aware of the reasons for the changes, and how they will affect the organisation and individual workers. There is more detail about communication in Chapter 7.

Loss of customer confidence

Like the workforce, customers may feel a level of fear when changes take place. Some may take their business elsewhere if the slightest amount of disruption to supplies or service is evident. This can again be at least partly overcome by communication. Letting customers know what is going on and, more importantly, selling them the benefits of the change is essential if customer service is affected in any way.

Loss of motivation

If change programmes are a frequent occurrence in an organisation, staff may lose motivation and general morale may be lowered. It is essential that this factor is overcome as this will soon start to affect the organisation in terms of poor timekeeping, absenteeism, decreased enthusiasm and efficiency that customers will soon notice, and reduced performance generally. This is a more difficult problem to resolve and will almost always require a long-term solution. This may involve a programme of different communications with staff and motivational events such as celebrations of good results, social events, 'away days' and so on. There is more about motivating staff in the next section of this chapter.

Loss of brand awareness

Changes to the organisation's product range or to packaging, etc. may have an impact on the brand. When customers are familiar with a brand and purchase it regularly, they may be tempted to try another brand if they do not like the changes that are made or are confused by them. Again, communication is the key to this problem. An extensive marketing campaign to reinforce the brand in its new image, for example, will help to achieve a seamless change.

Change will affect people – workers, customers, suppliers and stakeholders – in different ways. The key to a successful change programme and to keeping the non-quantifiable costs such as stress and loss of motivation to a minimum, is to communicate well so that the people affected by the change agree with, or, at the very least, understand the reasons for the change. People should always be given the chance to assist with the planning process and to be given information throughout the change process.

Motivating staff

One of the key elements of a successful organisation that looks for and works towards continuous improvement is a motivated workforce. We can all recognise when people are motivated and know that motivated people are willing and effective workers. We all know unmotivated people and have probably had the misfortune to work alongside one or two of them. Motivated people work harder. But what is motivation and how can we motivate ourselves and our staff and colleagues?

Motivation can be defined as the psychological condition of being motivated, i.e. having a reason for action. So, in order to motivate their workforce, managers will have to find a reason for them to work. They will have to ensure that members of their team know why they are asking them to work in a certain way and to make the objectives clear. This is, of course, easier said than done, especially as everyone is different, so there isn't just one thing that will motivate all workers. Everyone comes with an individual set of values and will work according to what is important to them personally. As always there are theories that will help managers to find their way around this problem. One such theory that is very popular is Maslow's 'Hierarchy of Needs'. He put forward his theory in 1943, stating that people have a list of priorities and that we would not seek to satisfy one need until we had satisfied more basic needs that were higher in priority. In order of importance his theory stated that these are:

1. Physiological needs – these include hunger, thirst, warmth and sleep. These needs, it could be argued, are a starting point for working for money. If we have an income then we can keep ourselves fed, have somewhere to sleep and so on, so they do motivate us to find a job and come to work but they will probably not be enough to make us work hard towards objectives set by our bosses.

2. Safety needs – these include peace, security and stability, so our jobs will provide these to a certain extent but again, not sufficiently to seriously affect our work objectives.

3. Love needs – this includes not just a loving relationship but also friendship, a sense of belonging and social acceptance. Again, work will provide some of these needs. Some people may be motivated by not wanting to let their colleagues down as they want to belong to a team.

4. Esteem needs – this includes the need for recognition, achievement, respect and confidence. This is where work really satisfies a need in that being set a target and then reaching it will certainly give one a sense of achievement and if achievements are rewarded then we will satisfy our need for recognition and so on.

5. Self-actualisation – this means making use of our full potential. Work is an important part of satisfying this need for many people. Making full use of all our skills and abilities in our work role will fulfil this need.

Although Maslow's theory does not give us a full explanation of motivation it certainly goes a long way towards helping us to understand how work can be motivating and how managers can motivate their workforce.

So what must a manager do?

From this explanation of motivation, we can see what a manager will have to do to motivate people to work towards the common objectives of the organisation:

- Give workers a sense of achievement – this will give them confidence in their own abilities, which is a key motivating factor.
- Recognise success – as we mentioned in Chapter 7, people do generally respond well to the publicising of work well done. It does not have to cost a great deal to recognise success, as simple schemes such as 'Worker of the Month' or a mention in a company newsletter can be enough to increase the level of motivation. Genuine praise will almost always motivate people.
- Promote people based on what they have achieved – this again gives people recognition and will motivate them. To be fully motivated, people need to feel that their hard work and success does not go unnoticed and in organisations where promotion, better jobs and training opportunities appear always to go to the 'next in line' or the person who shouts the loudest, the levels of motivation will be low whereas if people feel that if they work hard they will progress in the organisation then they will be motivated to put in extra effort.
- Give them satisfying work – this will increase self-confidence.
- Give them responsibility – the recognition of being given responsibility will motivate most people and will increase their levels of self-respect and confidence.
- Help them to work in teams – working in a cohesive, high-achieving team will satisfy people's need for belonging and social interaction. Being supported by colleagues is a hugely motivating factor in many people's working lives.

Obviously, having a job and a salary helps us to satisfy the higher priority needs in Maslow's Hierarchy. Contrary to popular belief a good rate of pay and shorter working hours will not necessarily motivate people in the long term although if a rise in pay or extra days off are presented as a reward for what has been achieved they will have some motivating effect.

What are the costs of not changing?

The main cost of not changing is falling behind. As every other organisation and also the world at large are changing around us, if there are no changes made within our organisation then there will be a number of effects:

- Competitors will introduce new products and take sales away with products that are more in tune with what the market demands.
- Regulations will change and leave the organisation open to legal consequences.
- Customers will become dissatisfied. There is a general expectation of continuous improvement and if customers perceive that there is a lack of interest they will look elsewhere.
- Staff will become demoralised. This can / absenteeism, poor performance and sta jobs with more go-ahead organisation: time, to a deterioration in the general workforce as the more able and con
- The skills of the workforce will bec
- Technology will move on, leaving It may become impossible to rep hardware (PCs, printers and th

of suitable spare parts, or to update or upgrade existing software. Ultimately, it will become difficult to find staff who are able to use the old technology efficiently.

● Production machinery may become defunct and, like computers, become impossible to repair. It will also become less efficient and will produce less and less of the product.

● Suppliers may stop making some of the products that the organisation has used for many years. This may include spare parts for machinery or the raw materials and components needed to make products.

As can be seen from the list above, there are many costs associated with staying where you are. In today's business world, continuous improvement and innovation is expected. Any organisation that does not 'move with the times' will ultimately not survive.

Assessing training needs

Training has been proved to be a way to improve a business, so there is a clear business case for investing in training people, especially when new methods or systems will be introduced. The benefits that an organisation can gain from training include:

● increased productivity
● increased profitability
● increased staff motivation
● increased customer satisfaction.

ough the benefits of training are obvious, it is vital that you a training needs analysis before setting up any training ld be unwise to commit to any of the costs or effort associated with training before considering what the organisation needs and what skills and aptitudes are already available. You must identify the gap (and there probably will be a gap) between what the organisation requires to carry out its change programme and what all the individuals are able to deliver in their various roles.

Changes of any kind may generate a need for training. The new areas that might need to be addressed include:

● changes in practice in your business area
● a new piece of machinery
● a new computer system or piece of software.

Any training that is arranged must suit both the need that has been identified within the organisation and the person who is to receive the training. In order to be able to fit the training to the new requirements, several methods can be used:

● a comprehensive staff appraisal scheme for the staff involved in the changes – if one is not already in operation
● job descriptions for each position in the department in which the change is taking place
● person specifications for each member of staff affected
● organisation targets – for profits and sales or output that will be affected by the change.

INSTANT TIP

You must know your business and your people. You must also be able to show that any training need that you identify during your training needs analysis can be linked to a specific business need.

Before you arrange or even recommend any training, you need to evaluate all areas of the organisation affected by the proposed changes so that you know exactly what you are trying to achieve. You need to understand where the organisation is going (the goals) and also how it is going to get there (the performance needed to reach those goals).

The gap between current performance and required performance is the one that you will have to fill with the help of your training solutions. So if, for example, one of the goals involves increasing sales by 50 per cent and the current performance of the sales team is static year on year, you will know that some training for the sales team and/or sales management is something to which you should give serious consideration.

Even after you have identified needs within the departments affected by the change and have conducted a thorough assessment of gaps in performance, it is still possible that training is not the solution. Do not be tempted to set up or purchase a training course for the wrong reasons. Training carried out for the wrong reasons will not solve your problems, nor will it make you a better manager simply for having given staff some training opportunities. If you waste money on the wrong course or training for the wrong staff, you will merely increase your problems – so make sure you know why you have opted for the training.

INSTANT TIP

Quite often finding out what training specific members of your staff need is easy – you could ask them what training they think they need!

Training objectives

Next you will have to list objectives for the training that will state what you want, and are able, to achieve. As always, your objectives must be:

- Measurable – decide how to quantify the improvement you want to see after the training has taken place. For example, if you think that a training course for your customer services staff is necessary, set a target for reduction in the number of customer complaints or returned goods, or an increase in sales totals in a specific area – whatever fits your business – and incorporate this into the change programme.
- Possible – can you afford the training that you are proposing? Will the results from a successful change programme justify the expenditure? Will you be able to release the relevant staff for the amount of time that the proposed training will take? Will the nominated staff be able to cope with the level of course?
- Positive – all goals and objectives must be stated positively. Your training objectives should encapsulate the goals that you have arrived at during your training needs analysis.

Also, remember that your training objectives must support the objectives of your organisation and the change programme. The primary purpose of a training strategy is to improve the performance of the business and should not be put into place simply to further individual development – even though this is a welcome by-product of training.

What suits best?

The next step is to decide what type of training will suit the purpose. If you have individuals who need help to fill skills gaps then external courses may be best. If, however, you have an entire team who needs bringing up to speed on something new that will be introduced into the department (for example, a new computer system) then it may be possible to organise training in-house. Alternatively, training may be readily available. This may be the case for new machinery, for example, when the machine's manufacturer may train a number of operatives for you as part of the purchasing deal.

Whatever training needs are decided upon, the costs – including the time spent by staff being trained – must be factored into the change programme's budget. And, one last thing on training, don't forget to monitor the results to ensure that you get what you pay for and also that the end results serve your purpose.

Monitoring costs

Monitoring costs involves setting standards and then monitoring performance against these standards and is an essential part of a manager's role. Standards that are set in order to monitor costs must take into account not only the cost of the resource but also the quality of it. So, for example, an organisation manufacturing car components would need to calculate the total cost of producing the part – including materials, labour, power etc. – and also ensure that parts of the correct quality are produced. If lesser quality parts are produced then this could result in a further cost – that of customer dissatisfaction or safety issues. If the factors of cost and quality are used to set standards then these standards can be used to measure costs and also used in calculating selling prices. Monitoring costs against these standards must be done continually and there is a variety of documents and internal systems already in existence that will be able to help with this task:

- Production records such as timesheets, rejection notes, overtime booked, standard production times – these will show what has gone on during the production process and will make it possible to calculate actual resources such as worker hours and raw materials used.
- Budget forecasts – the expected performance must be compared with actual performance to find out how good – or bad – the current performance is.
- Invoices for goods sold – has the organisation achieved the prices for the goods or services they are selling that were included in the original budget forecasts? If not, why not? Here, you would look for an extraordinary price agreed with a customer, perhaps a very large order quantity that was sold with a special bulk discount.
- Invoices for goods purchased – has the cost of goods purchased matched the forecast? Again, if not, why not? Have larger quantities than expected been purchased or a higher price paid?
- Manufacturing results – do the quantities that have been produced match the forecasted quantities? If fewer have been manufactured then economies of scale that were factored into the forecasts will not have had the desired effect and production costs may have increased accordingly.
- Annual accounts – these will tell you how much has been spent in a variety of areas including salaries and wages, purchases, overheads such as property rents and maintenance, and all these figures can be used to help a manager to see how actual costs compare with those predicted.

As always when considering monitoring anything, there is no point in measuring or monitoring if no action is taken when deviations or problems are uncovered. Corrective action must be put in place.

Controlling costs

A manager has a very important role to play in controlling costs. In effect, they will have to manage resources effectively and efficiently so that costs are kept to acceptable and forecasted levels. There are many ways in which resources can be managed, depending on the resource.

Time

As a worker, a manager will have to manage their own time and control the use of it. Time management is an involved subject and many books have been written about it, but the main way to good time management is to understand how you use it. This requires you to ask yourself some tough questions such as:

- How much time do I waste – on personal phone calls, chats and emails?
- Do I procrastinate, missing deadlines or working late to do what I should have done earlier?
- Are my priorities clear?
- Do I have a clear grasp of what is required and when I will be able to achieve it?
- Do we have too many meetings in the department or in the organisation as a whole and are meetings efficiently run?
- Do I delegate effectively?

The answers to some of these questions will not only help a manager to manage their own time but also ensure that employees' time is used to best effect. In addition, time can be managed by checking the time taken to do specific tasks in the department. This could involve using records such as employee attendance records and overtime sheets, machine productivity reports and production schedules.

Energy

Energy in the form of electricity or other power sources can be managed by taking simple measures in a department such as instructing staff to turn off lights or equipment after use, reducing waste and so on.

Materials

Although materials control is a bigger element of a production manager's work role, all managers will have some materials that they can control the use of. For example, a shop manager will need to control stock and sales materials and an office manager will need to keep a check on the use of stationery and so on. In all cases, the manager will have to ensure that materials are purchased at the right price, are used correctly, that the right amount is kept in stock and that theft is kept to a minimum.

People

This is arguably the most difficult and complicated resource that any manager has to control. As always, plenty of information will help in the control process. A manager will therefore have to know employees really well – what motivates them and what their skills and shortcomings are. The extra element in controlling people is good communication. Making sure that they know what is expected of them and what resources they have available to them will help to ensure good results.

Equipment

Most managers will have some equipment in their department that they will need to manage. This may be large manufacturing machines for production managers, tills for a retail manager and copiers, phones and computers for a manager in an office environment. In all cases, better results will be obtained when the equipment is well-maintained and also used properly. To ensure this a manager will have to set up and monitor a maintenance schedule and to provide the appropriate training for all workers who have to use equipment of any kind. Questions such as 'Is this machine fit for purpose or is a better, more cost-effective solution available?' will need to be asked on a regular basis.

Information

All managers have to deal with copious amounts of information and more efficient running of a department will be possible if the right information is used. To control information a manager will have to ensure that the information that is received is relevant, complete and accurate. If it is found to be lacking in one or more of these criteria, then the manager will need to insist that the supplier adheres to the standards set or find a new source for the information.

Money

Most managers – apart from financial managers and accountants, of course – will have little control over actual cash but they will certainly be able to exercise some control over what is spent in their departments. They could do this in a variety of ways according to the purchase: a sales manager could control what his sales staff claim on expenses, for example, and control their adherence to the rules or standards that have been set; a production manager could control wastage. More senior managers may also be able to make suggestions about investment decisions that affect their departments.

Controlling costs and the use of resources is an important task in any organisation and is a vital part of a manager's role. There are lots of different ways to control costs and the list above is simply a start on the quest to avoid over-spending.

Maintaining change

Continuous improvement must be a goal for every organisation. If organisations don't change and move forward then they will go backwards as markets change and events overtake them. Change is not something that can happen just once and then all the problems will be solved once and for all, so maintaining the change process is essential to the success of any business. Of course, there are some major changes that an organisation will have to carry out that will not need to happen again but, in general, improvement must be continuous, so after any change has been made a manager needs to be looking for the next necessary change. A programme of continuous change should ideally be in place that is regularly reviewed alongside the overall strategy for the organisation to ensure that the changes that are happening are taking the organisation in the right direction.

There are a number of methods by which change can be maintained. While there will always be resistance to change and many people will get to the end of a change programme and give a sigh of relief, hoping to sit back and live with the status quo for a while – the majority of people in an organisation will need some encouragement to keep going through many changes and through continuous improvement. It is therefore worthwhile setting up quality improvement groups and work improvement groups. Ideally, these groups should include workers from both inside and outside each department to take advantage of any cross-over of ideas between departments, plus senior managers who have the authority to allocate resources and to make things happen.

Communication must be aimed at convincing all members of staff that change will be ongoing and that there are valid, acceptable reasons for this. They must buy into the idea that every aspect of the organisation can be improved and made to work better.

SUMMARY

In this chapter about the costs of change, we looked first at financial costs and then at those costs that may not be quantifiable, such as stress, and the loss of motivation, customer confidence or brand awareness. Next we examined motivation using Maslow's Hierarchy of Needs which holds that we all fulfil our needs in order of priority. In Maslow's Hierarchy hunger is a top priority and gaining satisfaction from our work is one of the lowest. This helps to show how staff can be motivated to satisfy their needs for esteem and self-actualisation.

We then looked at the costs that would be borne by an organisation that resists change and neglects the need for continual improvement over a period of time. These included demoralised staff, finding that repairs and updates to software and production machinery become unavailable and dissatisfied customers.

Training is often necessary when making changes and we looked next at how to assess training needs. When changes to business practices, a new piece of machinery or computer system are introduced it will be necessary to complete a thorough review of the business and its people to ensure training suits the needs of all concerned. Training objectives must then be set that are measurable, possible and positive. As always, results must be monitored.

Next we looked at monitoring costs. Standards must be set and performance monitored against these using existing systems such as production records, budget forecasts and sales records. We looked briefly at ways to control the cost of resources including time, energy, materials, people, equipment, information and, of course, money.

Finally, we saw how change can be maintained and continuous improvement made by the use of regular reviews plus quality and work improvement groups.

ACTION CHECKLIST

1. Have you any personal experience of stress or loss of motivation caused by the need to change being neglected?
2. Consider how your own work role helps you to fulfil your need for self-esteem.
3. If you are currently going through (or have just completed) a change programme in your organisation, assess whether there are any training needs that have not been satisfied.
4. Think about the last change process that affected you. What costs were involved? Consider both quantifiable and less quantifiable costs.
5. Could you set up a work improvement group in your work area? What do you think it would achieve?

11

What of the future?

Any organisation that does not look to the future is not likely to succeed in today's changing world. Some changes – for example major economic downturns or natural disasters – are difficult, and sometimes impossible, to predict. No organisation can make itself future proof. However, by embracing a programme of continual improvement, organisations can help to safeguard their own futures. They can also ensure that their staff are well-trained and that they have everything in place to deal with whatever the economy may do or with other local, national and international events that may occur.

Key management challenges in a changing world

One of the most difficult tasks any manager or owner has is to maintain the stability necessary to maintain levels of production or to continue to offer services of the required quality amid the enormous changes going on in the world around them that cause intense pressure on businesses. These pressures include:

- Pressure from owners and stakeholders in the business – senior managers will always be pushing for better results and shareholders will always expect a return on their investment.
- Market pressure – the size or nature of the markets may change and plans may have to be revised. An organisation that has traditionally only had to deal with a local market will increasingly have to deal with global competition along with the different ways of doing business that modern communications have facilitated.
- Changing technology – this can have an effect, for example, on where an organisation is located. With the technology currently available it is becoming increasingly possible to operate some types of business just about anywhere and historical reasons for where a business is located may become irrelevant. Other areas that have seen enormous changes caused or facilitated by new technology in recent decades include production (where quality of products has been improved), customer service (where response times have been speeded up) and sales and management (where video conferencing can eradicate the need for face-to face-meetings).
- Global changes – this can affect the mix of a workforce. As an example, consider the availability of East European labour in the United Kingdom over recent years. Global changes can also affect financing, competition and the market.
- Political changes – some organisations will fare better under one type of political regime and worse under others, and when there is a change of government this change will have to be accommodated.
- Competitive pressure – increasingly competition can be from anywhere in the world. It can also come from different types of organisation. Some industries that, in

the past, have required high levels of investment to set up are now far more accessible to smaller enterprises due to changes in technology.

Whatever changes are going on in the organisation's market or in the world, managers will still have to produce results and to keep striving for continuous improvement. The changing environment has to be accommodated so that, for example, in a severe economic downturn, an organisation will have to strive to keep on track despite the results of recession, including restrictions on credit from their lenders, falling sales, rising costs and ever-changing interest rates. The changes and difficulties caused by these external influences will have to be dealt with and the strategy and results of the organisation maintained. It may, however, be necessary to amend targets or, in extreme circumstances, to change direction. For example, if the strategy of the company for a programme of expansion depended heavily on financing being available and an overdraft facility was withdrawn when the economic climate changed, then the expansion would have to be reviewed. Other sources of finance would have to be found or the expansion plans scaled down according to the finance currently available.

Although all these changes increase the pressure on organisations, there will always be a need for change within the organisation and for continual improvement. It is an ongoing battle to maintain direction and to keep achieving successful change amid changes that may be totally outside the organisation's control.

Can you predict changes?

The changes that have been seen in the past few decades may be a guide to what could be expected in the future. Changes in unemployment, for example, will continue to happen in the years to come and this will present changes for any organisation in that the right personnel may become easier – or more difficult – to recruit. Recruiting and developing the right people as and when needed is the only antidote to this uncertainty.

There are a number of areas where changes may occur and where effective management will avoid problems in the future.

Trends should be looked for, noted and acted upon. These may be found in the following areas.

Customers

It is possible to anticipate customers' changing needs by looking at past records, listening to what they are saying and knowing the market in which the organisation operates. Changes in the customer base can also be predicted by looking at trends. For example, has the profile of the organisation's average customer changed from young married couples to older people? Or from large multi-national companies to smaller organisations? Keeping a close eye on what competitors are doing will also help to spot trends – more on competitors later in this section.

Methods of production

Any manager involved in production should take an interest in new types of machinery on offer and in the methods being employed throughout the industry. This can be done by attending relevant conferences and exhibitions, reading trade magazines, dealing with suppliers, networking with others involved in the industry and researching specific types of production on the internet. Using these methods, any manager can find out about developments in their area of interest. This will apply not only to the machinery used to produce goods but also to methods of quality control, supervision and performance improvement, and to the technology used.

Technology

This is one area where great advances have been made in recent years and there is no reason to think that these changes will not continue. Keeping up to date with changes in technology and understanding the effect they may have on the organisation and the benefits they may offer is essential.

Competition

It is rare for any one organisation to be the market leader and always to be first with new developments and products, so it is essential to observe competitors closely. Are they offering new products? Or attacking new sectors of the market? Or are they taking on new sales or production staff? Whenever they do something new or seem to be taking a particular direction, it is good to ask why and to assess the impact on the market. Is this something other organisations should follow and will it gain customers for competitors at the expense of other organisations? Obviously, if several competitors start to go in the same direction then a trend is developing and this can be an indication of what the future holds.

Creating the future

Regular reviews of what has gone on in the past in an organisation and also how world events, such as economic downturns, have affected the organisation can be a starting point for building an organisation with a future. Scheduled strategic and business reviews should be a part of every organisation's routine. The gathering and management of information is crucial to an organisation's future success. With the right information an organisation will be able to:

- analyse levels of risk
- reduce uncertainty
- predict the outcome of taking different actions
- maximise the chances of success
- minimise the chances of failure
- assess the strength of competition
- plan for the future.

Planning for the future is something that every organisation should be continually doing. It involves analysing information, coming up with new ideas based on that information, ruling out ideas that will not work and then deciding upon changes that will be advantageous to the organisation. Done regularly and thoroughly, planning for the future is something that will enable an organisation to keep on the path it has chosen.

It is important to note that whatever plans have been made, they must be kept flexible. Sticking to plans in the face of drastic changes taking place outside the organisation can be a severe mistake. The way to keep a high degree of flexibility in plans is to continually review both the plans themselves and the external situation. It is important to know exactly what can affect the organisation's ability to fulfil its plans. So, for example, a thorough grasp of what competitors are doing and what customers want is essential in maintaining a competitive edge in a changing market.

INSTANT TIP

Don't simply make a plan and then stick to it but review it at regular intervals, taking changes both inside and outside the organisation into account.

Some organisations do, however, thrive in a changing environment. They do this by developing a deep understanding of their markets and by continually reviewing the situation they are in, assessing how changes will affect them. This can result in an increase in expertise within the organisation when managers learn how to respond quickly to changing customer demands and to develop a flexible approach to sales and production. Staff may become more stable, loyal and productive if they are given the right encouragement and reassurances in uncertain times. Taking advantage of the opportunities that external changes will invariably present is the key to survival and success in difficult times.

SUMMARY

Although no organisation can future proof itself, it is possible for organisations to take action that will help to safeguard their futures. Regardless of the changes going on in the world around them, organisations have to maintain stability and keep up their change programmes to ensure continuous improvement. The external changes that may affect them include market changes, political and economic changes, and changing technology.

We looked at how organisations may be able to predict future changes by examining information from various sources to pinpoint trends.

Another way in which any organisation can try to control its future is by regularly reviewing its performance and by planning accordingly. However, it is important not to be too rigid, sticking to plans when it is not appropriate, as it's then impossible to take advantage of the opportunities that external changes may present.

ACTION CHECKLIST

1. List three specific changes that have taken place in the past few years that have affected your organisation.
2. What sorts of changes would affect an organisation's stability?
3. What information would you use if you were trying to find a trend in the market in which your organisation operates?
4. What risks do you consider that your organisation currently faces?
5. Can you think of an example of an organisation that is thriving in a changing environment (or has, in the past)?

12

The Companion Interview: John Tusa on Managing Change

The following interview with Sir John Tusa was conducted by Ed Peppitt, author of *Six of the Best* (Hodder) just as Sir John came to the end of his time as Managing Director of The Barbican Centre. During his 12 years in the role he led a huge and successful programme of change to the culture, architecture and infrastructure of the much maligned Centre. The changes attracted widespread approval and brought back to life a tired institution, illustrating in very real terms how change can and should be managed successfully. As Ed Peppitt says, Sir John took it from being 'universally unloved' to a 'thriving and diverse arts complex' in a restored Grade II building.

Sir John is currently Chairman of the Wigmore Hall Trust, a Vice Chairman of the British Museum, a Trustee of The Turquoise Mountain Trust Foundation, Chairman of the Court of Governors for the University of the Arts, London and Chair of the Clore Leadership Programme.

Ed Peppitt writes:

Sir John Tusa is a British television journalist and manager of arts and broadcasting organisations. Having presented *Newsnight* on the BBC from its inception in 1980 until 1986, he went on to become Managing Director of the BBC World Service (1986–1993).

Since retiring from his BBC World Service post, he has been critical of some BBC policies. He deprecated the former director general John Birt's focus and management style and has been outspoken about subsequent decisions to pare down World Service activities in Europe.

Since 1995 he has been Managing Director of the Barbican Arts Centre in the City of London. He is also Chairman of the Board of the Wigmore Hall in London.

He is the author of several books, including two written jointly with his wife Ann Tusa: *The Nuremberg Trial* (1983) and *The Berlin Blockade* (1988). John Tusa's most recent book is *Engaged with the Arts: Writings from the Front Line*.

He was educated at St Faith's School, Cambridge, and at Gresham's School, Holt and then at Trinity College, Cambridge, before joining the BBC as a trainee in 1960. He was awarded a knighthood in the Queen's Birthday Honours list in June 2003.

At the time I had arranged to meet Sir John Tusa, the Barbican had been the subject of a lot of press attention. It was about to celebrate its twenty-fifth birthday, and is also nearing the end of a spectacular £30 million refit. In fact, the future of the Barbican looks rosy, with an ever more diverse arts programme, now managed and co-ordinated centrally.

It hasn't always been like this. Ten years ago the Barbican was in crisis. The Royal Shakespeare Company (RSC) moved out, staff morale was as low as it could be, and as a venue, the Barbican had been described as 'universally unloved'. Whoever was recruited to take over as managing director, the principal objective would be simply to survive.

The man they chose for the job was John Tusa, a BBC news journalist, author and former Managing Director of the BBC World Service. Together with his Artistic Director, Graham Sheffield, he has transformed the Barbican into the thriving and diverse arts complex that it is today.

I could see straightaway why he would make a great subject for a chapter of a book about managing change. First of all, though, I was keen to learn about why he had taken the role on. What sort of person relishes the challenge of rejuvenating a universally unloved arts complex? What qualities did he think would be required? I wondered whether he had appreciated the extent of the challenge he took on?

Change is a fact of life, and in business we are all called upon either to manage or to endure substantial and sustained organisational change. Every week, another commentator argues that the organisations that will thrive in the next decade are the ones who continually adapt their offering in line with a constantly changing marketplace. If we are to thrive as managers, we need to harness the skills required to manage change effectively. Who better to offer us advice but Sir John Tusa?

The pace of change

I began my discussion with Sir John Tusa by referring to a quotation from the Chartered Management Institute. It read:

> *'It is widely accepted that the pace of change has intensified in recent years. The impact this has had on the organisational landscape in the UK has been matched only by the effect on individuals.'*

I asked Sir John if he agreed that the pace of change had intensified, and about the impact of change.

Yes, I suppose it has. Why do I sound slightly cautious about it? I think as far as the arts are concerned, theatre is theatre, music is music, classical music is classical music. On the other hand, when you look at what we were doing in the concert hall ten years ago, it was by and large the orchestra and nothing else. And yet within the last ten years the use of combination art forms, such as orchestra with video, is now far more accepted. It is not every orchestra, nor every concert, but it is much more common. So the sorts of things that go into concerts have changed. For example, we have just had a Steve Reich Festival. I wouldn't say that would have been unthinkable ten years ago, but it would have been highly unlikely. And that was almost all multi-form. He has written two operas accompanied by DVDs with video clips. That is certainly a change that has occurred in the last ten years.

And so what you are staging has changed over the last ten years?

Yes, and the way in which artists express themselves has changed. Now artists use the orchestra, they use electronics, sampling, video and live movement. This has developed over the last ten years, there is no question about that.

What has caused the change? Is it a result of the technology that has been made available? Has that provided another art form to exploit, if you like, or do you think it's the changing demands of audiences? Perhaps it's both?

I think the technology has come first. Artists have got interested in it, and then developed their expertise in it. At the same time the audiences, who are also technologically aware, have followed. I think it is probably that way around, but clearly if you didn't have an audience that was also technologically sophisticated, they wouldn't turn up to experience it. On the other hand, there are lots of people who still only want a concert, who only want a play, and they don't want it messed around with. Or who just want nice drawings and paintings, who don't like video art.

But there is an increasingly significant audience which does like it. And all that has really certainly changed at an accelerating pace over the last ten years. To give you one idea of how big the change has been, ten years ago the Royal Shakespeare Company were our resident company, and that's what the Barbican was known for. It was Shakespeare. Then they left, and their audience left with them, because that was what they were interested in.

Ten years on and we have Simon McBurney and Complicité and his last show, *The Elephant Vanishes*. And people were queuing up the stairs to get in. It was a very different audience. That was a production which was extremely radical in its use of things like video, film, lighting and how the production was done. So I think that the pace with which that sort of production has developed over the last ten years is very real.

Opportunities for change

A lot has been written about the Royal Shakespeare Company's decision to move out of the Barbican almost ten years ago. I couldn't help but imagine that this must have come as something of a blow to the recently recruited Managing Director. What went through Sir John Tusa's mind when he discovered that his major resident company had decided to 'part company', so to speak? How does the effective leader react to a situation like this?

Do you think that the RSC moving out of the Barbican presented an enormous opportunity for you? Did it provide a catalyst for change?

Well it was certainly a catalyst. Everybody told us that we couldn't manage. So, yes, it was a huge catalyst and an opportunity, and we certainly wouldn't be doing the sort of things that we do now, or anything like them, if the RSC were still with us. So it was a huge change and a huge opportunity.

Essentially what we have done is to realign the approach to all the arts from being 'small c classical' and 'small c conservative', to arts which are much more engaged with the newer available forms of expression. I reckon that if you were to look at our Arts Diary from ten years ago and compare it with today's, it would be absolutely unrecognisable.

Can I wind back the clock a decade or so to 1995? Back then, the Barbican was described as 'crisis-ridden' and 'universally unloved'. What made you think, from your own career perspective, that the Barbican was the right opportunity for you?

There were two things, one comparatively defensive and one not. At the time, I was working in BBC television news, and I knew I had reached an age where my shelf-life in front of the camera was very limited.

Also, reading the news was alright, but it wasn't terribly stretching, especially having led the BBC World Service for six years. So I had been vaguely keeping my eye open for an appropriate challenge. Because the Barbican is a multi art-form centre, rather than an opera house, a concert hall or an art gallery, I thought this was probably the only one that I had any authority to manage. And so when it seemed to be imploding and crisis-ridden, I thought I had very little to lose. I knew I needed to move and I was very lucky that that happened when it did.

I'd really like to know what it was like for you. You take over a crisis-ridden Barbican. Where on earth do you start? What is the process for looking at what needs to be changed, both in terms of the scale and its impact?

I don't believe that anybody who goes into an institution ever has any real idea of what the nature of the problems are. I think everybody goes in, to one degree or another, fairly ignorant, or else they are kidding themselves. I think that's probably necessary, because if you knew everything that was wrong you would probably conclude that it was too great a challenge!

I believed, and thank goodness I was right, that the basic finances were alright. The revenue budget was fine. Beyond that, once I got in and met the senior directors, I just knew immediately that the set-up I inherited was not going to work. The atmosphere – in terms of how people behaved, the sort of things they said, how they argued, and the general cultural atmosphere – was completely negative and sterile. There was also a great deal of back-biting and in-fighting.

And do you think that this attitude had created the crisis in the first place?

It had both created it, and it had been created and made worse by it. Either way, it was very, very bad. And some of the people who were reflecting or expressing this atmosphere were people who had been appointed by the previous incumbent, which was worrying. So I knew within six weeks that at least two of the senior people had to go.

As soon as that?

Oh yes. So I said to the City of London Corporation, 'I cannot work with A and B'.

And if there is some core advice I could pass on, it would be this. Don't think that you can put up with people. If you can't work with them, and I mean really can't work with them, do not hang around. Don't kid yourself that things are going to get better, or that you can do something about it. Once you know that, you have simply got to move on. And that was easily the best thing that I did.

And what effect did that have on the wider staff? I understand that morale was not at its highest at that point, anyway. So what effect did that actually have?

Well the short-term impact was that they assumed there would be even more blood-letting. When I made the first change, I knew there was going to be a second, so that needed some careful footwork. So there was a certain assumption that heads were going to be rolling, and that was something we just had to get through. Once three months passed, and then six, people realised that it was *not* a cull of all of the senior management. But those six months were just something that we had to go through. I knew that once we had different people in that it was going to work differently. And I think that when I appointed new people, the staff understood, and could see for themselves, that these were different kinds of people. First, the new people were competent; second, the new people were open; and third, the staff could begin to sense that the atmosphere among the directors was changing for the better.

In fact, of my six directors, four of us have been together for ten years. And the remaining two have joined within the last five. So we've been very stable, and whilst you might say that stability itself has its own problems, it is a very different order of problem. But once people could see that the team was there, and that the team was open and settled, then morale started to improve.

Another change was that we started to introduce open staff meetings. Surprisingly, it had never happened before. Never. When we announced the first staff meeting, morale was such that many saw it just as an attempt at a short-term fix. I remember asking somebody after the meeting what they had thought of it and they said, 'Well it's all very well, but it won't happen again, will it?' I had to assure him that it would happen three times a year. Most people were fairly dubious at first, but we did it, and we still do it. So that was also another very, very important milestone.

You mentioned earlier that people questioned whether the changes to the senior management team were part of a wider cull. I think you said that in a situation like that, you have just got to be open and honest about what is happening. Would that be right? What advice would you give a company director who knows that they have got to go through that change themselves in their organisation?

Well given that I knew that there was one other person who still had to go, I had to be careful what I said when the first person came and asked if there would be any more. I had to use rather political machinations and just hope that the time between change one and change two was not so long that it would damage relations even further.

So with something like that I think there was no alternative but to be cautious and not to sound too evasive. But I think I could say quite openly, 'This is not the start of a wholesale programme'. There isn't any easy way, but above all, what you *don't* say is, 'No, no, no, that's it', when you know that something else is going to have to be changed.

About three years later there was quite a lot of further change, but that was for different reasons, because having got the directors right we then knew that the place could only be run properly with a lot of co-operation from the departmental heads. They, by and large, took the view that they had a job to do, they had a job description to fulfil, and that was what they did. So when invited to contribute in a much broader way to the running of the centre, and to make it a broader, more imaginative contribution, most of them either couldn't or wouldn't, and with some it was the latter. They just weren't interested, and boy we tried!

Presumably some of those department heads had spent many years fulfilling their role in a particular way?

Yes, I think so, and nobody had asked them to look at the organisation in a broader way, and nobody had suggested that their contribution was not just to do their job but to think much more broadly about what they did. So, as a board of directors, we realised that this wasn't working. We had tried to share the roles and responsibilities with the department heads, but they weren't interested. But that process itself was useful, in the sense that quite a number of the department heads chose to leave over the next year or so anyway. There were only a few that we had to part company with. We then recruited a completely new tranche of about 15 departmental heads, and forged a new relationship with them, which is the very open relationship that we have now.

Presumably you were looking for a very different type of person when you were recruiting the new department heads?

Yes, absolutely. We wanted people who were, of course, technically excellent, who were also good managers and who were people who were ready to contribute to the broader vision of what the Barbican was about.

Planning change

I was intrigued when Sir John mentioned that he hadn't appreciated the extent of the crisis at the Barbican when he took on the role of leading it. I wanted to know how soon it was before he did realise, and how quickly he developed a plan to do something about it. I wanted to know how much planning went into the change programme at the Barbican, and what the strategy was. Who was involved? How was the plan received? What obstacles stood in the way?

I think you began by saying that when you arrived at the Barbican in 1995, you didn't appreciate the extent of the crisis. At what stage did you start to form the vision of what the Barbican could, and should, be like? At what stage was the plan developed?

I remember in the first six months setting out a timetable for how all the facilities needed to be revamped. It set out a programme of everything that needed to be changed and how we planned to do it. And I remember presenting it to my committee, who are the supervisory board, and I could tell, even as I was doing it, that this was just water off a duck's back. They were never going to fund it. They didn't take it seriously. This was just not what the place was about. It was a complete waste of time.

So then slowly we realised that they would never 'buy' a strategic plan. We were helped by the fact that the building was getting older and all sorts of bits needed replacing. It always seemed to be the air-handling units! So at each stage we argued that there was no point spending £2 million on air-handling units in the theatre if you don't then also take the opportunity to do other things as well.

Once that process began, as a matter of fact in the theatre, the next time it was easier to make the same argument about the concert hall, the art gallery, and so on. So when you look through what's happened over the last ten years there was one major project more or less every year. When you look back on it, it looks like a deftly structured ten-year programme of change. True, it was very pragmatic, but it was driven by a very practical sense that this had to be done, firstly, and while we were doing that, we had to improve the facilities. So there has been a kind of super-pragmatism to it.

Then I suppose there was a stage when we had improved all the facilities, when we realised that we had to do all the bits in between. For example, the foyers, the new entrance, and all the other areas that are where the value was going to be added. So by that stage, and that's probably only about four years ago, it was then clear what the remaining elements of the strategy ought to be.

And these final changes are what have created the impression that the Barbican is a single arts complex, rather than a theatre, a concert hall, a gallery and so on?

If that's the impression, then that's terrific! That is what it was intended to do, of course. But although we knew that an enormous amount needed to be done, we also knew that the nature of the funding was such that there was no point in asking for a single, large sum of money. The Corporation would have just freaked! So there was, I suppose, a tactical canniness on our part. We have made the changes to the Barbican in bite-sized chunks, driven by practicality and necessity.

And presumably that's why you chose not to close the Barbican during any development phase, but to keep virtually everything open at all times.

Yes, because that would have been too much of a risk. The organisation was too young. If we had suggested that we needed to close for a couple of years, it would have killed the programme of renovation and innovation stone dead. So that was a very deliberate strategic position. We would soldier through, because even with bits of the place filled with scaffolding and hoardings, the art was still going on, and the arts were still evolving.

So that was a very important position – and over ten years, the arts were transformed, the building has been transformed, the way in which the organisation was run has been transformed, and I suppose there have been three conveyor belts running at slightly different speeds, but they are always running in exactly the same direction, and in the end all of them now, I think, are about where we wanted them to be.

You described the regeneration of the Barbican as a series of tactics, and in a way the arts and performances have evolved from an opportunity created by the Royal Shakespeare Company moving out. I get the impression that there was a lot of chance involved in the process. What role do you think you have played in this series of tactics and chance?

That impression of chance would be misleading!

Well I rather expected that was the case.

My key relationship has been with Graham Sheffield, the Artistic Director. From the time the RSC left, Graham said that we had to have a new kind of theatre, a new kind of programming. It would be international, so there would be a number of visiting companies, and it would be multi art-form. So the development of the arts was driven by that very strong vision – there was no chance involved in that.

I think that as far as the music programming was concerned, our core was the London Symphony. Then when the BBC Symphony was brought on board, that extended the repertoire by about 50 years, roughly. Then in our own programming, the Great Performance was doing the Baroque and the high quality international, so that also fitted. Then our relationships with promoters such as Cyrius gave us another element. Admittedly, there was an element of the opportune with the BBC Symphony. They came to us because they were being indifferently treated at the Festival Hall. Our music people realised what this would add. It wasn't simply another resident orchestra, it was an associate orchestra which was doing a completely different type of artistic programming, so it gave our music programme coherence just as the theatre programme had coherence.

Then by the time we took over the art gallery, which was only six years ago, we looked at what we were doing in the theatre and music, and asked ourselves what was the equivalent in the art gallery? That needed quite a shift, but now, in the last 18 months, I think we are there, and so the gallery programming is going to have a similar kind of feel.

Do you see the South Bank arts centre as your chief rival, your chief competitor?

Yes, it must be. But it is a very different beast because it is a coalition of independent units.

But surely that's how people regarded the Barbican ten years ago?

That's right, yes. And now we have much more artistic editorial control over what we put on in all the venues. That has changed, and that is best shown in the amount of box office risk. Ten years ago it was about £600,000, and now it's nearer £7 million. So that reflects the amount of artistic control, input and risk that we have now.

The impact of change

Organisational change affects people. It's generally accepted that some people handle and manage change better than others. From a personal perspective, I have worked with some people who relish the chance to change something, to try something new, and with others who live in constant fear and dread of the next change to be cast upon them.

There have been a number of studies into organisational change recently. The last Chartered Management Institute poll, for example, revealed that 89 per cent of managers had experienced some sort of organisational change in the last 12 months, and more than 50 per cent had experienced more than three major changes over the past year.

I wondered how Sir John Tusa viewed the way that organisational change affects its people? What lessons has he learned about reducing the impact of change on people? Sir John had already described the need simply to endure the culture of suspicion at the Barbican whilst changes were being made to the senior management team. But what about the changes whose impact was felt by the remaining Barbican staff?

I asked Sir John if he believed that organisational change was just a part of running a business?

Yes, but as far as structural change is concerned, we have only had two. Only twice have we had a significant reorganisation of some divisions. That's still plenty though!

Otherwise, the key areas of the arts division and its structure have been pretty stable. So have our people been subjected to change? Apart from what I have said about the way in which the arts themselves change, I'm not sure that they have.

I suppose people handle change in different ways. Some people just can't deal with change, whilst others take it in their stride and some even thrive on it. You come across as someone remarkably comfortable with the changes that you have made and the processes that you have introduced. Is that fair?

That's because I've made them!

But even implementing change presumably causes stress. Are you someone who suffers from stress?

Oh I thrive on it. Parts of what we've done have been stressful. Mainly, I would rather call them *interesting*. What I do dislike is having things which don't work. The frustration of something which is clearly not working is very much greater than the incidental stress that may appear from implementing a change. The two big reorganisations that we have had, have come from my colleagues. I've been aware that they have been needed, but the real push has come from my colleagues. Rightly or wrongly, that is how it has happened. But it hasn't been me saying, 'Right, we're going to do something different today. We're going to create this, that and the other'. So I think that suggests that there was an organic need for it.

You've got 250 people at the Barbican. When changes are implemented – whether they are programming changes, structural changes or development of the physical structure of the buildings – a lot of people find any change very, very stressful. How do you motivate 250 people to have faith in you, come with you, keep going, live through the change?

Well the important thing is that most of the change, and the need for the change, is first of all understood and identified at quite close to operational level. Take, for example, the services division. That's everything from the people who tear the tickets, to the bar and catering and so on. The need or the wish to change the quality of service came from within that division. I was only vaguely aware that certain things didn't work. But they are driving the change.

Now that is not to say that there weren't a lot of people who have had to change the way they work. That is true. But it has not been a top-down thing. It has been a need for change that has come from within the particular operational area, and when the change has been announced, and we have all said this is going to be difficult, this is going to be sensitive, this is going to upset people, the reaction of at least half the people, and sometimes more, has been, 'Thank goodness you've done it!' So, far from staff finding that sort of change difficult, it actually liberates them.

So they would say that you listened to them?

Yes. That makes the stress much easier to bear. The stress comes from being run inefficiently, or being run rigidly. You know that you want to be providing a different kind of service at a different level, but the rigidities prevent you from doing it. That's where the stress is. The liberation is when you get rid of that.

So how did your approach compare with the way you ran the BBC World Service? From a cultural perspective, was there not more of a hierarchical structure at the BBC which would have made the open way that you have managed the Barbican almost impossible?

I think the BBC World Service was 2,500 people: Many more layers, many more departments, and 50 nationalities, which added another dimension. Change is actually easier at the Barbican because it is smaller, and once you have identified what the vision and the mission are, and they are all consistent and coherent with what people believe, then change becomes much easier to deliver, because it is coming from inside. I think that was never quite the situation at the World Service. I have probably forgotten how difficult it was.

An organisation the size of the Barbican can be quite light on its feet. I mean the Barbican, and the people there, is a rather clever institution. And that cleverness is distributed and stored very widely.

You mentioned that the two organisational changes that you have implemented achieved what was intended. Would you have known along the way that they were heading in the right direction? Would you have known if it was working, or if something was going wrong?

Oh it was very clear. The fact that I needed a bit of persuading that the change was necessary sometimes meant that it was probably introduced a little bit later than my colleagues would have wanted, but what that certainly meant was that the reasons for making the case had become really apparent and the case been made. So in each case, it was very apparent by the time the change was made that it was going to work.

So what is the biggest change you have made at the Barbican, the one that has had the greatest impact?

How people behave and how we treat people. It's as simple as that.

OK, if I was a Barbican employee ten years ago, and I survived the changes and had grown with the Barbican under Sir John Tusa, what would I notice now? How would I be treated differently now?

There is much more information on an absolutely regular and systematic basis. So you would know that there is a monthly staff letter, you would know that there are three-monthly staff meetings, monthly core briefs, and an annual AGM, which we have just had. That's where I reviewed the last ten years, the last year and then the next five years. So the atmosphere is completely different.

There is much less sense of hierarchy. There is a much greater sense of responsibility. We are constantly pushing responsibility downwards.

Presumably that means much more reliance on the integrity and skill of the team leaders?

Oh yes. And there are some comparatively junior people who take big decisions. For example, our web designer. In hierarchy terms, she is relatively low down, but she is an absolute genius web designer, and if you consider that our face to the world shines through that website, then that is a fantastic degree of responsibility. But nobody worries about that. Nobody questions why such a junior person is carrying that amount of responsibility. She is just so good at her job that you would be a fool not to give her her head.

All those things you would notice as having changed from ten years ago. It's just about how you treat people, how you talk to people. From our point of view, it's all terribly simple. I think it's not being frightened of being open. There are a lot of organisations which are really frightened about openness. I will just give you one example of this. We are planning a book about the twenty-fifth birthday of the Barbican. We need an article by a theatre critic about whether the RSC was right to leave. And people said, 'Do you really want to air that?' And I replied that if we didn't air it, then someone else will. I'm not frightened of the answers. Some of our lords and masters over at the Corporation were almost panic-struck at the thought! My view is that it's there, it happened, it was a crisis – it is a part of the history.

Communication and culture

Many of the techniques, and much of the advice Sir John Tusa had offered for managing people through change seemed to centre on the importance of communication. Yet he had not used the word 'communication' once in our discussion. I wondered whether my attempt to group together these tools under this single banner was being too simplistic.

You describe the procedures that you have introduced as very simple. The staff letters, the staff meetings, the core briefs. They all seem to be about communication?

Yes. It goes hand-in-hand, side-by-side, with the view of how I treat people. It applies formally, and with face-to-face communication as well. We needed the formal methods of communication because some of my colleagues needed to learn that there was nothing frightening about being open as well. So I think that is something that I personally brought in, and that also comes from (a) being a journalist, (b) having come to management very late and (c) having done all these things for the BBC World Service as well.

I was going to ask you about that. You have introduced massive changes in 11 years at the

Barbican, but you lived through even greater cultural change at the BBC throughout the 1980s and early 1990s. How do they compare?

I think what I did at the BBC World Service was very similar to the Barbican, except that when I took the World Service over it was not in a state of crisis. It was a great institution which was waiting to have a lot of latent energy released.

Were you aware of that at the time?

Oh yes, and I had been aware of that from the outside as well. Equally, there were a lot of people at the World Service who were perfectly happy to go on doing what they had been doing for the previous 20 to 25 years, and thought that that was all that needed doing. But the challenges were the same, in the sense that you needed to have the right directors, and you have to look at your staff and identify the ones who are just running on autopilot and the ones who are capable of managing and editing in a more contemporary and imaginative, human way. And so that process took place at the World Service, just as it has taken place at the Barbican. But I suppose there was a really big challenge to get the organisation to start thinking about itself, and what it wanted to be. As it was a much older institution, it had its history, it knew what it did, it knew what it had done, it knew what its past was about. But it wasn't as good at knowing what it *wanted* to be, and what needed to change in order to become that.

Now, it is perfectly obvious that the way I approach change could not be more different from the way in which change came to the BBC under Director-General John Birt, after I left. That was a much more top-down system, which, as you well know, was regarded as not being the way you run that sort of institution. But there are others who were there at the time who say that a lot of necessary change was introduced. All I can do is to express and speak up for the style of change management which goes with the institution's standards, with the human values of people, and which I believe also expresses the sort of person that I am. So I think it is important to *like* people quite a lot! I think that bosses don't always give the impression that they do.

Given that John Birt's successor, Greg Dyke, couldn't have been *less* of a top-down person, do you think that Greg Dyke was better suited for the role?

Oh yes I think much, much more so, because he understood what the BBC's values were. I think that one of the really important things about transformation is that you, as the chief executive, must have an idea of the sort of organisation you have come to run, but you then need to understand the sort of organisation that it actually is. You may have an outside view, but you also need to discover what the inside view is, and then put those two together. Changes may be required, but if what you are doing is running completely across the internal value systems, then you are in big trouble.

At the Barbican, it took a little time before we thought we were in a position to devise what our vision and mission was. It was there, it was latent, but it wasn't ready. It was only when we felt that it was ready to articulate that we then went through that process. But it was certainly not a question of marching in and announcing what the organisation was going to be, what the vision and the mission were, and telling the people to get on and do it.

So had the vision for the Barbican never been articulated before?

No. It was very difficult to articulate a vision when so much of the art that you put on was not under your control. The art gallery was run by someone else. The RSC ran the theatre, and by and large what we did in the concert hall was fairly minor. It was only when we had got control of the arts programming that we could consider, and then articulate, what we genuinely stood for.

Is that control over the arts programming what the South Bank Centre still lacks? Is that the distinction between the South Bank and the Barbican?

Yes, I think that has always been the distinction, and I think that that will continue to be seen as the distinction.

It's interesting to see how our department heads, and others, see the distinction between the South Bank and the Barbican. They regard us as rather lean and sharp, and of course we are actually very broad-based. We are very diverse, we are not elite at all, and we are a bit experimental, radical even. So I think if you asked many of my senior colleagues if they thought the word 'cuddly' applies to us, they would say absolutely not! We aren't cuddly, we do not want to be cuddly, and by and large those are the values which are being expressed at the South Bank.

Looking to the future

Sir John Tusa is in an unusual position, insofar as he has already announced his retirement, and the search for his successor has begun. I wondered whether he could look back at the changes he had introduced and see a pattern? Is he proud of what his tenure achieved at the Barbican? What sort of person does he think should replace him and what advice would he offer them?

So the Barbican's twenty-fifth anniversary is next year – 2007? Are you proud of the Barbican, and what it is now?

Hugely!

I understand that the recruitment of your successor has already started. What sort of person do you think would be effective?

Well I think it needs to be quite a searching process, and probably quite an uncomfortable one. It's tempting to assume that there is nowhere obvious to go now, because people say we run the best arts programme in the world. My view is that just because you are the best, it doesn't mean that you can't get better.

So let's imagine that it's the middle of July next year and your successor has been identified. It's only charitable to take him or her out to lunch. What advice would you offer them?

You have to have the big vision for five years, and you have to stand up and say it, and you say it to everybody. Otherwise they will assume that everything is just chugging along in exactly the same way. After all, it works so well, why do we have to change? You really have to question what you need to change and why, rather than just sit on your laurels.

So your advice to anyone who needs to implement change would be to communicate?

Oh yes, communication is absolutely essential. You cannot go back on things like that. Communicate, and also delegate. You see, the interesting thing is that some of the departmental heads here are now almost fulfilling directorate roles, and they are certainly showing director-type behaviour.

It sounds as if, whilst the approach to implementing change is relatively straightforward, the institution itself has remained as complex now as it ever was?

Well nowadays there are so many more opportunities for what you can do. For example, our relations with all of our neighbouring arts institutions are now much richer. We are probably going to integrate the administration with the Guildhall School of Music and Drama; we may even end up in a full merger in two or three years' time. Then there's the whole question of how we relate to the 2012 London Olympics, and that's another big, big subject.

In other words, the opportunities in all the things we are working on mean that a really ambitious strategic growth is now possible. It wasn't possible ten years ago because we were struggling to survive.

I read a quotation of yours, that 'Management is all about asking questions rather than answering them'. We've looked at many of the skills required to manage change in an organisation, but presumably you would add that you need to have the ability to question the need for change in the first place?

I think that's right. Funnily enough, at the end of my recent presentation to staff at our AGM, I said something quite similar – I said that it's not shameful to miss targets, but it is an error not to set them. And that's what my successor must do. As I said earlier, we couldn't do that ten years ago, because our only mission was to survive. But because of where we are now, we need some very bold targets and vision.

You must be very anxious about who will be recruited to succeed you?

The other day my assistant asked me if I minded who my successor was. I only thought of the right answer yesterday. I should have said, 'I don't mind, but I do care!' I don't mind in a possessive way, but I will care if they balls it up!

Conclusions and recommendations

Before meeting Sir John Tusa, I had read an article in *The Times* which had described his 'effortlessly powerful presence'. 'The word "gravitas"', the article continued, 'could have been invented for Sir John Tusa'. The journalist who wrote the article had been absolutely right. It's not difficult to see why people are prepared to listen to what he has to say, and to follow him willingly along the path that he chose for the Barbican Arts Centre. His combination of calmness, dignity and charm – which makes him such a fascinating person to talk to – is matched by his eagerness to actually get up and get going with the job in hand. That, I believe, is why every organisation would want to turn to Sir John Tusa in a crisis. Plenty of leaders can offer you sane and pragmatic advice. Sir John is one, but he would also harness everyone's support and commitment, make them feel completely in control of the situation, and then get on with dealing with it.

Sir John's legacy is a formidable one. He has transformed the Barbican in his 11 years as Managing Director. Together with his Artistic Director, Graham Sheffield, he has recreated and relaunched the entire performing and visual arts programme. All this, while every venue at the Barbican, from the concert hall to the theatre and art gallery, has been redeveloped and improved.

So how has it happened? Sir John's own view is remarkably straightforward: 'I have simply set a course, knowing that my colleagues will deliver.' It clearly has not been as easy to deliver as it has to describe. In an interview with *The Telegraph*, he described the Barbican he entered as 'a shambles. Nobody trusted anyone. It took four to five years of slowly grinding things through before we began to feel it was anything other than immensely hard work. I was on a three-year contract and I can tell you I thought very hard about renewing it.' Once the scale of the challenge had sunk in, the reality of what has happened involved earning the trust of his people, sharing the vision with them of what the Barbican could be, and then involving them in the process every step of the way.

As with so many effective leaders, part of Sir John's leadership success can be attributed to his energy and passion for the arts. He is known to work very long hours, but admits that he doesn't regard what he does as work, rather as 'sheer pleasure'. His passion is such that when his tenure at the Barbican was extended by 18 months, it seemed almost like a reward for his ten years of hard work. After all, it will ensure that he will see through the final phase of redevelopment, and then be around to join in the Barbican's twenty-fifth birthday celebrations in March 2007. In his own words 'this will mark the completion of everything I have wanted to achieve for the institution'.

Managing change checklist

If you are considering change for your organisation, or are leading a team of people through change, here are some issues to think about. You might want to find a few, valuable minutes to take a clean sheet of paper and jot down any ideas that the following list generates.

Be aware of change around you

Is your organisation adapting to the changing needs of your customers or marketplace? In what ways are your customers changing their behaviour? What mechanisms do you have in place for keeping track of what your customers or stakeholders want?

How do you view change?

If a crisis occurred in your organisation, would you view it as an opportunity or a catastrophe? What would be the equivalent of the RSC moving out for you? What would you do if your biggest customer went elsewhere? What steps can you take to ensure that you treat a challenge to your business as an opportunity for change?

Managing conflict

Are you kidding yourself that things are bound to get better? What are you putting up with? Is it time for you to take some brave but necessary decisions in order to move forward?

Being open

Where do the ideas for change originate in your organisation? Is change being driven by your staff, your customers, or your senior management team? To what extent do you involve your staff in the strategic change process? What are your staff telling you needs to be changed? Are you open and honest with your staff about the need for change, and its likely impact on the people concerned?

People and change

Do you view a member of staff leaving your organisation as a problem, or as an opportunity to review your requirements? What can you do to minimise the stress and unease that strategic changes cause? Have you always kept lines of communication open with your people? What roles and responsibilities can you push down to your more junior staff?

Planning change

Are the changes you plan to implement a series of tactics? Are they part of a wider strategic plan? How would you know if a specific change you have made is having the effect that you planned? Can you measure the effects of the change? Who are the key colleagues around you whom you can rely on for support?

Culture

Do you think that you need to consider changing the culture of your organisation? If a client or customer walked into your office or building, what impression would they get of you and your organisation? Would they think that it looks like a great place to work? What changes do you need to make? Where do you plan to start?

Your biggest change

What is the biggest change that you have ever had to make? What could you have done better with hindsight? What lessons have you learned?

National Occupational Standards

This book covers the NOS Management and Leadership standards – Facilitating Change. The following table will help you to locate these competencies in the book.

Competency	Unit no.	Chapter	Chapter title
Encourage innovation in your team	C1	2	What is change?
		3	When is change needed?
		4	Where will you get ideas for change and innovation?
		5	How can you introduce change?
		6	How can you manage change?
		7	Why do people oppose change?
		8	How will you know if the change has worked?
		10	What are the costs of change?

Encourage innovation in your area of responsibility	C2	2	What is change?
		3	When is change needed?
		4	Where will you get ideas for change and innovation?
		5	How can you introduce change?
		6	How can you manage change?
		7	Why do people oppose change?
		8	How will you know if the change has worked?
		10	What are the costs of change?
Encourage innovation in your organisation	C3	2	What is change?
		3	When is change needed?
		4	Where will you get ideas for change and innovation?
		5	How can you introduce change?
		6	How can you manage change?
		7	Why do people oppose change?
		8	How will you know if the change has worked?
		9	Do you have to abandon current methods?
		10	What are the costs of change?
		11	What of the future?

Competency	Unit no.	Chapter	Chapter title
Lead change	C4	2	What is change?
		3	When is change needed?
		5	How can you introduce change?
		6	How can you manage change?
		7	Why do people oppose change?
Plan change	C5	3	When is change needed?
		5	How can you introduce change?
		6	How can you manage change?
		8	How will you know if the change has worked?
		10	What are the costs of change?
Implement change	C6	6	How can you manage change?
		7	Why do people oppose change?
		8	How will you know if the change has worked?
		10	What are the costs of change?
		11	What of the future?

Further information and reading

Useful organisations and websites

Chartered Management Institute
Management House
Cottingham Road
Corby NN17 1TT
tel 01536 204222
www.managers.co.uk
For information about all aspects of management and management qualifications.

Management Standards Centre
3rd Floor, 2 Savoy Court
Strand
London WC2R 0EZ
tel 0207 240 2826
www.management-standards.org/home

Department for Business Innovations and Skills
Ministerial Correspondence Unit
1 Victoria St, London SW1H 0EY
tel 0207 215 5000   www.berr.gov.uk
For information about all aspects of business.

Official UK Government website www.direct.gov.uk
For a wide variety of information including employment and education.

Office of Fair Trading www.oft.gov.uk
For information on legislation affecting businesses.

Institute of Chartered Accountants in England and Wales
www.icaew.co.uk
For information about KPIs.

Chartered Institute of Marketing www.cim.co.uk
For information on marketing, customer service and using KPIs.

Marketing UK www.marketinguk.co.uk
For information about market reports.

BSI British Standards tel 020 8996 9001

Business Link
tel 0845 600 9006   www.businesslink.gov.uk
Business Link is a government-funded network of local advice centres for business.

Chambers of Commerce www.chamberonline.co.uk
Local Chambers of Commerce are good sources of information on a variety of local and national business matters.

Investors in People
helpline 0207 467 1946   www.investorsinpeople.co.uk

Microsoft Small Business Centre
www.microsoft.com/uk/smallbusiness
For information about software that will help with collecting and analysing customer information.

Design Council   www.designcouncil.org.uk
For information about product design and innovation.

British Retail Consortium   www.brc.org.uk
For information about retail selling.

Institute of Business Consulting
helpline 0207 566 5220

Learndirect   www.learndirect-business.com
For advice about all sorts of business training and courses.

Market Research Society   www.mrs.org.uk
For information about market research.

Research Buyer's Guide   www.rbg.org.uk
For information about market research agencies.

Association for Project Management (APM)
www.apm.org.uk   tel 0845 458 1944

Small Firms Enterprise and Development Initiative
www.sfedi.co.uk   tel 0114 241 2155

Department for Innovation, Universities and Skills
www.dius.gov.uk

Useful reading

Adair, John, *Decision Making and Problem Solving* (CIPD) 1999

Baguley, Phil, *Performance Management in a Week* (Hodder & Stoughton) 2002

Baguley, Phil, *Teach Yourself Project Management* (Teach Yourself) 2008

Barker, Stephen and Cole, Rob, *Brilliant Project Management: What the best project managers know, say and do* (Prentice Hall) 2007

Bird, Polly, *Teach Yourself Time Management* (Teach Yourself) 2008

Burnes, Bernard, *Managing Change: A strategic approach to organisational dynamics* (Financial Times) 2004

Cameron, Esther and Green, Mike, *Making Sense of Change Management: A complete guide to the models, tools and techniques of organisational change* (Kogan Page) 2009

Hayes, John, *The Theory and Practice of Change Management* (Palgrave Macmillan) 2006

Kemp, Sid, *Quality Management Demystified* (McGraw-Hill) 2006

Peppit, Ed, *Six of the Best – Lessons in Life and Leadership* (Hodder Arnold) 2007

Portny, Stanley E., *Project Management for Dummies* (John Wiley & Sons) 2006

Walmsley, Bernice, *Teach Yourself Training* (Teach Yourself) 2005

And other titles in the Instant Manager Series

Index